It's a Jungle Out There, Jane

It's a Jungle Out There, Jane

Understanding the MALE Animal

Dr. Joy Browne

 Crown Publishers NEW YORK

Copyright © 1999 by Joy Browne

Published by Crown Publishers, 201 East 50th Street, New York, New York 10022.
Member of the Crown Publishing Group.

Random House, Inc. New York, Toronto, London, Sydney, Auckland
www.randomhouse.com

CROWN is a trademark and the Crown colophon is a registered trademark of
Random House, Inc.

Printed in the United States of America

Design by Barbara Sturman

Library of Congress Cataloging-in-Publication Data
Browne, Joy
        It's a jungle out there, Jane : understanding the male animal /
    Joy Browne . — 1st ed.
        1. Men—Psychology.   2. Men—Humor.   3. Masculinity.   4. Sex role.
    5. Man–woman relationships.   I. Title.
    HQ1090.B76   1999
    305.3—dc21   99-36230
                                                                 CIP

ISBN 0-609-60357-4

10 9 8 7 6 5 4 3 2 1

First Edition

For all the boys and men who have enriched my life,

from my dad on. Y'all have broken my heart, lit up my life,

darkened my door, called, not called, loved wisely, well,

or incompletely—hopefully you will see yourself in these

pages and know you made an impression. I can only hope

the feeling was mutual.

CONTENTS

Introduction

T HE ONE THING I know for certain is that you're all going to
be mad at me. Men who read this will think that I'm bash-
ing 'em, while women will say I'm letting the guys off the
hook. Well, that's okay. Let's all just take a deep breath. This book
isn't about black and white, right and wrong, men versus women,
married versus single, or straight versus gay. And this book certainly isn't about being politically correct. This book is about evolution. It's about exploring the evolution of male behavior, from the
primordial ooze to the postcoital snooze and everything in between.

This book is about understanding where men are really
coming from so we can all understand where to go from here.

Whether it's an ancient fertility figure drawn on cave walls
with exaggerated breasts and hips (yeah, we all know what's em-
phasized in the male of the species) or biblical references to the
Garden of Eden where Eve is fashioned from Adam's rib (no, you

can't tell a male skeleton from a female skeleton by counting ribs; believe me, I've tried) or a nursery rhyme that suggests that girls are made from sugar and spice while little boys are made from puppy dog tails, the differences between men and women have always been stark, but they've never been more profound or irritating than they are today. And it doesn't matter that we seem to be moving toward equality in the workplace, the voting booth, the cancer ward, the locker room, and even the dressing room. Let's face it—men and women aren't the same. Duh. But what are the *real* differences? Where did they come from?

Since NASA has proved there are no little sperm pods on Mars, we all must be from the same organic material on *this* planet, so let's start right here on Mother Earth. Let's start by talking about our biological ancestors, near and far. Let's look at the maleness and femaleness of the animal kingdom, the nature part of the nature/nurture equation, opposable thumbs, upright posture, straight legs (the only primate that's got 'em), and significant loss of body hair (though you should see some of the guys I work with . . .) through the prism of biological, psychological, and social evolution.

That's what this book is about. By starting with the easy stuff—the biology—we can learn how other mammals organize taking care of their young, dealing with sex, dividing labor, growing old, competing, and bonding. And maybe learn something about ourselves from our observations. Then it's time to move on to the really complex stuff: social organization and mores and—*whew*—language and expectation and romance and mother-in-laws and kids and nostalgia and high-school reunions. That's when we may learn something about ourselves.

The real evolution that causes us humans to stumble isn't biological (that stuff makes glaciers look speedy), it's social. When you really get down to it, the automobile, phone, caller ID, E-mail, the Internet, and the Pill (especially the Pill) have done more to change the face of social evolution than the millions of years preceding the last thirty or so. Men and women are getting closer together in terms of size, weight, stamina, and strength than males and females in any species ever. And we're having a tougher time getting along than ever before. It's not coincidental. So this book starts with the obvious—the biology—then proceeds to the history of human behavior, then gets to the really interesting stuff: How do we evolve from here so we can meet each other's needs while still being true to ourselves? How do we socially and psychologically evolve *today* so that our biology and history is served and channeled and able to create a foundation for the next gazillion years?

The answer starts here: We're all animals, living beings capable of spontaneous movement and rapid motor response to stimulation. So yeah, men are animals. So are women. Even after 4 million years of evolution, our biological natures can smack us upside the head with surprising subtlety and frequency. Add sociological conditioning and wham! The sperm hits the egg. The XX female starts planning her wedding and the XY male starts planning his career. Well, not exactly . . . but truer than not.

Even though we stand upright, greet each other with a smile instead of a sniff, and wag our tongues instead of our tails, we're still animals in an instinctive, primal center that influences how we feel, act, and react. Particularly in group interactions, there are a lot of similarities between animal and *human* animal behavior. Whether we're talking about gorillas in the mist or guys in suburbia, it's best to study organisms in their natural habitat to understand what's really important. This requires keen observational skills, an open mind, and patience. Exploring the male from *his* biological, sociological, psychological, and anthropological point of view is the crucial first step in truly understanding him.

This book can help you understand why guys act, think, talk, love, make love, stay, stray, tune out, tune in, and turn on the way they do. And, oh yeah, why they don't help much around the house. Tarzan, that means that when you get to the last page, you'll know yourself better than you do right now. And, Jane, if you're with a guy, know one, or gave birth to one, you'll be able to answer the question "Why did he do that?" armed with the latest information on genetics, hormones, brain differences, neonatal variations, and socialization from birth and beyond.

This isn't a book about finger-pointing ("See, men really *are* beasts!") or what's right and what's wrong. It's simply about what *is*. About what's going on with the male half of our species. About understanding, not underscoring; about comprehending, not censuring or celebrating.

Listen, if we can figure out the answers to the questions about male behavior, we can stop effortlessly misunderstanding each other, getting angry, looking to blame, telling our friends, and carrying that chip around on our fragile or not-so-fragile shoulders. In short, we can stop fighting like cats and dogs and learn to appreciate and cherish each other.

Quantum Leaps

E VOLUTION IS both slow and linear. Most relationships can't wait around for evolutionary changes. What we're mostly looking for is *revolutionary* change. That requires quantum leaps that work, not aberrations that lead nowhere. We're talking survival here. Each chapter will contain *quantum leaps*, starting from how male animals are and leading to the way they might one day be. There are also steps that show how the man himself, or the woman who would like to love him, might act as a catalyst to this leap. In general:

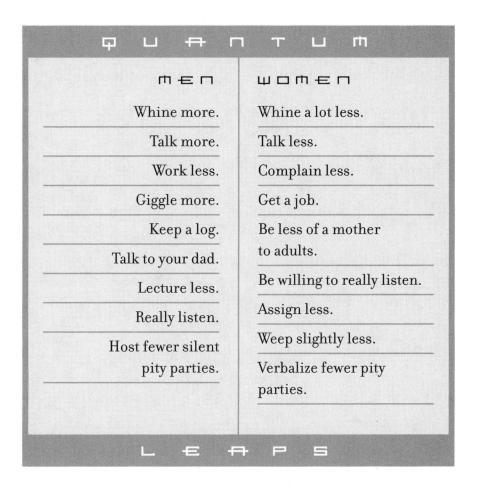

QUANTUM	
MEN	**WOMEN**
Whine more.	Whine a lot less.
Talk more.	Talk less.
Work less.	Complain less.
Giggle more.	Get a job.
Keep a log.	Be less of a mother to adults.
Talk to your dad.	
Lecture less.	Be willing to really listen.
Really listen.	Assign less.
Host fewer silent pity parties.	Weep slightly less.
	Verbalize fewer pity parties.

LEAPS

It's a Jungle
Out There,
Jane

One

The Jungle

Men and Work

A DAY IN THE LIFE of a male baboon is one long struggle for status. Only dominant males breed. They get the girl, eat the best food, enjoy gazing out over the savannah while other baboons groom their coats. It's a good life . . . if you're troop leader. For all the rest of the males, it's a life of envy and plots to overthrow the number one guy. A young male baboon continuously attempts to gain status by approaching dominant males and flashing his deadly canine teeth. If an elder flinches and retreats, the studly young baboon moves up in the world. If the dominant male displays bigger fangs and greater fierceness, the Alpha wanna-be turns on his heels and bares his backside in defeat.

A day in the life of a human male is one long struggle for status. The most successful guy gets the cover girl, the expense account, the corner office. He has minions to cut his hair, tailor his Armani suits, shine his Bruno Magli shoes. It's a good life . . . if you're CEO. Less powerful males feel that life is about getting ahead, beating the competition, making the sale, garnering a promotion, scoring a bonus, or just keeping younger, hungrier predators off their derrieres.

In this country, when a man is between the ages of twenty-five and fifty-five, his identity is primarily defined by what he does to earn a living. Ask a man to describe himself and he'll tell you what he does. Ask a woman and she'll tell you her marital status. It's not that one is bad and the other is good, it's just that they are quite different. Not only does a guy live through his work, his work is who he *is*. To a man, the world of work is a jungle—a teeming, exhilarating, dangerous, frightening, proving ground. The law is survival of the fittest. The rat race is unrelenting, and whether you're dealing with government regulations, a cranky boss, a stubborn customer, or a competitor, it's a dog-eat-dog world. For a man, what he does is who he is.

The male animal's—*any* male animal's—drive to dominate is a powerful primal urge. Nowhere is this more evident than in the human jungle of the workplace, where guys are constantly looking for ways to brandish their fangs, gain status, cover their butts, become top dog. The beginning of understanding men is understanding how men act *at work*. When it comes to the adult male of the human species, the way to gather the most relevant data in the shortest time is to study him on the job, whether that's at an office, a construction site, a sales territory, a train engine, or a tractor.

Yeah, women also hack their way through the nine-to-five jungle, work the room, the land, the firm, but there's a major difference: Men *define* themselves through their work. A man without a job is a bum; a woman without a job is a *wife* or a daughter with some guy supporting her. While men may also be dads, husbands, lovers, beer buddies, racquetball players, or amateur auto mechanics, the idea of being out of work feels like dying. Everything stops—the familiar world disappears. *He* disappears as his reason for being seems to vanish. (Even from a genetic standpoint, if you can't stick around to protect and provide for your offspring, what's the point in bringing them forth?)

Understanding men at work means understanding dominance, aggression, and status. For most men, working is not just about making a living, it's about gaining and maintaining status. Interestingly, the word *status* comes from the same Latin root as "statura," meaning "upright position or body height." The original definition of *status* is "the way one stands." A guy feels his status is quite literally the true measure of himself as a man. His *stature.* His *state* of being.

Men have been taught that aggressive behavior will elevate their status at work. Aggression has a long history of being a prerequisite for successful men. Shareholders want a killer, not a CEO who's "understanding."

One of the Fortune 500's giants, Maurice "Hank" Greenberg of AIG Insurance, was dubbed A.I.G. for Aggressive Inscrutable Greenberg by his *friends.* Think what his competition called him! Another giant on the list, Jack Levy, managing director of Merrill Lynch's Mergers and Acquisitions, says his secret to success is "Never let the other guys breathe." Look at recent best-sellers on the business bookshelf: *Trouncing the Dow, Eat the Rich, Winning Every Day, Unleashing the Killer App.* What's this mean? Guys feel they need to "go for the throat" to succeed at work and achieve the status that goes with being the head honcho. Men are threatened by younger, more successful men, since these are the young lions who can smell weakness and obliterate an aging animal's manhood in one masterful swipe. The most dominant male wins . . . and winning is everything.

Winning can be fun or confusing or even important for women, but winning is crucial for men. Women rarely invest as much self-worth in the outcome. Losing doesn't feel life-threatening to a woman, just disappointing. When a man loses, he feels beaten, whipped, emasculated, humiliated—destined to spend his life *grooming* the winners, eating leftovers, and never, ever getting the girl.

Guys assert their dominance at work all the time, often without even realizing it. They stand instead of sit, they "bark" orders to coworkers, they "forget" to do something their boss asks them to do, they undercut another's achievements.

Stella, twenty-three, called my radio program to complain about how uncomfortable she was with her boss's behavior. She was working as a legal secretary for one of the junior partners in a large Chicago law firm. Whenever she had to go into her boss's office to discuss a case or take dictation, he leaned back behind his desk, both feet up, both arms stretched behind the back of his head. "Like I *want* to stare at his armpits!" she said. While she wasn't sure why it bothered her so much, she wanted to figure out some way to make him stop.

This is a classic example of dominant male behavior. There's even a name for it: the chest thrust. It's a throwback to an Alpha male's puffed-up posture (out-jutting chests) in his attempt to appear larger. If you've ever seen a picture of a silverback gorilla pounding on his chest to frighten away challengers or intruders, you've seen the chest thrust at its most basic.

Stella's boss is consciously or unconsciously trying to impress and intimidate her with his manly size. He may also be subconsciously trying to sexually stimulate her with the primal scents from his sweat glands. Before you get all persnickety about armpit ardor, consider this: Have you ever worn your boyfriend's unlaundered shirt or snuggled up to a recently vacated pillow? What you're doing is tuning in to that old animal part of our brains that connects smells and emotions. Pheromones (those chemical substances that are produced by an animal to stimulate a behavioral response in individuals of the same species—sort of turn-on tonics) are the basis of the modern perfume industry's multibillion-dollar sales. See, men aren't the only animals on this bus!

Most guys unconsciously puff up all the time at work. To emphasize their size, they stretch, fluff up their hair, spread their arms open wide to make a point. It's their way of saying, "I'm the boss" or "I'm more important than you" or "Even though you outrank me, you don't scare me." Once Stella understood what was going on, she was able to relax and feel less threatened. I even suggested that she just imagine feeding him a banana. (Hey, no Freudian snickering here!)

The constant battle for dominance at work means that men keep score. It's crucial to understand that their scorecard has only two columns: Success and Failure. There's no column for "I tried." Trying but not succeding is failure with a pretty ribbon tied around it, but it's still failure. For men there is only *doing* and *not doing.* Trying but not succeeding is failing, and failing feels like death. This "scorecard" mentality dates back to their childhoods. Boys grow into men with the sense that "big brother" is always watching. Big brother is, of course, *Dad.* He's watching, judging, scoring, measuring, making sure his son measures up. That's how life feels to most men. Even guys who grow up without a father in the home feel as if there's a "dad" somewhere, watching, always on the lookout.

And when men grow up, when Dad passes away, when the father figure no longer figures as part of their daily lives, the universe takes over as "Dad" with a fat red marker checking off their successes and failures. To guys, it feels as if somebody is always watching and judging.

If you're a guy, work can feel like a daily battle for survival. It's important to hide vulnerabilities and never let anyone see you sweat. For the wolf to be banished from the door, the walls must be thick, the larder filled, and the fire stoked. To a modern man, the fittest doesn't necessarily have the biggest biceps, but the biggest brain, the wiliest manner, the smoothest patter, the largest office, the most powerful mentor, the most important client, the most aggressive temperament.

Animal Instincts

MALE ANIMALS at work in the wild can tell you a lot about human male animals at work in a company. Take a pack of African wild dogs. The pack operates like a corporation. The Alpha male is the CEO, the Beta is the VP, and the Omega is the guy in the mailroom. Of course, there are more than three wild dogs in a pack and more than three employees in most companies. In both, however, there's usually one head honcho and a bunch of wanna-bes.

When wild dogs are at work—say, stalking a gazelle—each animal has a job to do. The Alpha leads the hunt by targeting the prey. The pack members then fall into formation, isolating, chasing, flanking, and ultimately bringing the gazelle to its knees. Once the prey is weakened, the Alpha goes for the throat. It's a communal effort, with a communal reward, though no one pretends it's a community of *equals*. The Omega wild dog would never dream of getting first dibs on a fresh kill any more than the Omega mailroom guy would expect to have lunch in the executive dining room. Everyone knows his place.

Wild dogs work to be promoted for the same reason that men do: The top dog gets the top girl, the best food, the best sex. That's why Beta VPs seek every opportunity to show the gang they're worthy of the top spot. If the Alpha lets his guard down, the Beta is ready to draw first blood faster than you can howl at the moon. The competition is fierce and the most aggressive dog wins. But the risks of an attempted coup are great. A wild dog who loses a leadership battle may be banished from the pack altogether, rendered a literal lone wolf, left to fend for itself—in essence, a wild dog out of work. Being "out of work" means scrounging for leftovers and spending Saturday nights alone. It's a lonely, lousy way to live.

This "pack mentality" permeates the human workforce. Guys dream of being top dog, of taking over the company and running things "right." But the fear of failure and the primal need to be part of the pack keep many guys locked in their "Beta" or "Omega" positions. That doesn't mean they stop competing. Instead, they may pick a less confrontational mode of "competing," such as bad-mouthing the boss behind his or her back, or boasting about how they could do it better. This is a way to *safely* flex their muscles. They can be king of the sandbox without venturing beyond the backyard.

This makes men feel powerful without feeling frightened. Most men would rather dare ulcers, high blood pressure, or a blown aorta than admit *fear.* Fear is unmanly. The fearful man is the class nerd who never gets picked for the team, rather than the macho hero, leader of men. He's the waterboy rather than the quarterback. Fear is for wimps. Therein lies the rub: While most men are driven to compete, the mere thought of losing feels incredibly scary. And denying that gut-churning, anxiety-provoking, middle-of-the-night fear doesn't make it go away.

All of which means, if you happen to be a boss or involved with a boss, you've seen how great it is being the Alpha male dominating the Omegas, maintaining his power position. But when an Alpha feels overwhelmed at times, he can begin to doubt his manliness. And the easiest solution to this feeling of being overwhelmed is the one that's hardest to do (a dichotomy that comes with the territory). Most women know instinctively that the best way to ease this sort of stress is to enlist subordinates as advocates for the good of the company, firm, force, or team, instead of treating them as adversaries or competitors for your prized position. This means seeking their opinion, appreciating and acknowledging the work *everyone* does. The best bosses make their employees feel cherished and valued, which creates employees who *want* to follow their leader. One of the reasons that women are making the strides that they are in the workplace is that this is their natural tendency. If you see your Alpha male causing himself more stress than necessary, perhaps you can help him sort out whether the threat is real or not. (Or if your boy's a Beta, perhaps you can suggest a better sort of coup!)

The truth is, most guys go to work with the sense that they are one paycheck away from disaster, and if (when) it strikes, the whole family will be on the deck of their own personal *Titanic*. Even if there is money in the bank, a pension plan or the promise of a golden parachute, a family inheritance or a working wife, the *feeling* is one of imminent potential disaster. Men dine out on horror stories of guys who've had it all, then crashed. Whether it was their granddaddy who took a header out of a high window in the stock market crash of '29 or a college roommate whose windows don't open but whose margins got called during a recent Dow Jones tumble and is now selling used cars for his father-in-law or the exec at a large corporation who was downsized into a three-year "sabbatical," what your guy sees is a living death.

Our capitalist society has done a horrifyingly effective job of convincing men that they are worth what they get paid. The belief that the best man wins is ingrained, ubiquitous, and intense.

WILD THINGS

Q. *Which animal is the most ferocious hunter?*
    a. Elephant
    b. Hyena
    c. Lion

A. *Hyena.* It's a myth that hyenas only lurk in the shadows and scrounge for tidbits after a more powerful animal's kill. In fact, hyenas are fierce hunters, killing two-thirds of their own prey. The lion, a.k.a. "King of the Jungle," actually scavenges for food more often than the hyena does. (Male lions spend a whole lotta time lounging around the veldt *looking* predatory.) And elephants, of course, are vegetarian. The point is, in the animal—as well as the human male animal—world, image is *everything.* It doesn't really matter if you *are* dangerous as long as everyone thinks you are and treats you with respect. Maintaining an image of strength and invincibility is what helps males, of all species, survive.

Q. *Which position of a wolf's ears indicates that he's ready to attack?*

    a. Forward

    b. Backward

    c. Straight up

A. *Forward.* Body language is as crucial in animal communication as it is in human communication. The posture of a wolf ready to lunge is ears forward, tail down, head low, and haunches crouched. Jackrabbits who spot such a posture nearby know instantly that their days are numbered. Ears plastered backward indicate submission and fear. Erect, straight-up ears and posture communicate confidence and pride. It's the same with human animals. Standing straight, holding your head high, and keeping your chin up indicates the type of self-assurance and competence that inspires confidence and keeps predators at bay.

Q. *In the shellfish community, which attribute indicates a dominant male prawn?*

    a. The size of his claws

    b. The color of his claws

    c. The thickness of his body shell

A. *Color.* Blue claws in a prawn clan are the ultimate status symbol. Young males have orange, delicate little claws that molt and toughen as they ascend the social hierarchy. *Big* blue claws are the best. But, as with humans, size doesn't always matter. A male prawn's true colors are what make him a manly man.

Boys to Men

TO UNDERSTAND the man, it's crucial to look at the boy he once was. Most American boys share one common trait: They are trained to be aggressive from *birth*. Male aggression and dominant behavior is a part of our culture. Boy babies are called "strong" and "tough." Girl babies are called "sweet" and "soft." A recent survey done at Oregon State University found that adults tagged strong primary colors like blue, green, and red as "boy" colors, while pink and lavender were labeled "girl" colors. Parents decorated their kids' rooms accordingly. Boy Scouts have 119 Merit Badges, ranging from Archery to Wilderness Survival. Girl Scouts have badges, too, but are more widely known for their cookies. Little boys play with *Power* Rangers, *action* figures, video shoot-'em-up games—toys that encourage them to aggressively ferret out the enemy and destroy it.

Take a look at some of the latest male-targeted video games on sale at Toys "R" Us: WWF War Zone, Tenchu Stealth Assassins, Resident Evil, Duke Nukem: Time to Kill. Boys' toys are about black and white, good and evil, strong and weak, friend and foe, winning and losing. Good guys and bad guys are sharply defined. There are no "sorta icky" guys who come from broken homes and have low self-esteem. The bad guys are over-the-top *baaad*. Video battlegrounds are so violent, they make live war footage look tame by comparison. In Toyville, the enemy is vaporized, annihilated, eradicated from the universe. And there are never any sobbing widows or fatherless children.

Toy wars teach little boys how real wars should be conducted. War is hell, but good soldiers get the job done. They seek and destroy. They don't think about the enemy's feelings or being "fair." War is about winning, and winning is everything. It's an act-now-feel-later (if at all) existence. Feelings get you labeled a coward or cause battle fatigue or post-traumatic stress disorder. The idea is that "good" soldiers are much less prone to such "disabilities." These are the subtle and not-so-subtle messages little boys are bombarded with while growing up.

Another notion boys are taught is that competition is essential. Competing is a part of a boy's everyday life. They hang out in "packs," skirmish daily for the top-dog position. Watch boys on a school bus—it's a scramble for the best seat. Or watch two guys walk down the street—invariably, one will leap up to tag a street sign or an awning, then the other will try to jump a bit higher. Organized sports is a breeding ground for competition. Boys play sports. Watch sports. Talk sports. Girls compete, too, but it's a whole other animal. Girls on the soccer, football, and baseball fields is a recent (and still rare) phenomenon.

When girls do suit up with the guys, the primary gripe from their male teammates is not about private parts in the locker room, but the notion that a girl will lower the standard of play. She'll undermine the team's ability to *compete.* She'll get them branded "losers." The same with women in the military ("She'll crumble in combat"), the boardroom ("She can't play hardball"), the police department ("The bad guys will outmuscle her"), or any other mostly male stronghold. Or men fear that a woman will be a sexual distraction, using her wiles to render them helpless (no sex, please, it'll deplete precious bodily fluids). Competition—in all its guises—rules. Take a look at *The General's Daughter* to see all of these factors brought to violent life in John Travolta's interpretation of Nelson DeMille's take on women in the military.

Suzanne, thirty-four, who is trying to raise an enlightened, politically correct six-year-old son, called recently in frustration. "I don't allow him to play with toy guns or weapons of any kind," she said. "No violent video games or bloody action figures. I buy him neutral, peaceful toys. Male and female dolls. Stuffed animals. Building blocks. Books. Musical instruments. Yesterday I walked outside and was horrified to see Jeremy aiming a slingshot at a bird perched in the jacaranda tree in the backyard. He'd rigged it using a rubber band attached to Barbie's two splayed legs. He was using one of his building blocks for the projectile. Aaargh!"

Jeremy told his mother that his friend Bobby had shown him how to do it and dared him to try it. So he tried it. In his little-boy way, Suzanne's son was asserting his manhood. He was proving his "manliness" to his friend, and his dominance over his mom and the defenseless bird. I'm not suggesting that boys will be boys and nature has a stranglehold on Suzanne's little cherub. Most behavior is learned and can be unlearned. But it's a mistake to underestimate the power of the social forces that shape us. A few play dates can undo years of careful molding.

Growing up, boys are viewed as much more dangerous than girls. They have to be watched. Their behavior must be monitored. A parent has to keep track of them or heaven knows what they might get themselves into. With females, the real threat of youth is pregnancy. With guys, it's violence, getting someone pregnant, doing drugs, burning down the house, beating up Dad, or inventing some new disaster that boggles the mind. Guys are perceived as much less under control. Curfews are instituted primarily due to the threat of the male—to keep girls *in*, as much as keeping guys off the streets. It's not so much that girls will do bad things, it's that boys will do bad things to girls.

A lifetime of sexual stereotyping reinforces the notion that boys must be ready to rumble at all times. Conquering. Winning. Beating chests and pummeling the competition.

A friend of mine—a male—recently said, "Have you noticed how women become like men once they go to work?" I replied, "What a male thing to say!" In his opinion, women aren't becoming independent, creative, self-reliant, goal-oriented team players, and good managers. Nope. They're just becoming *men!* I don't think so. Possessing a penis isn't a prerequisite for cool, business-like, or productive behavior in the workplace, thank you very much. Women can learn the rules and adapt them. But my friend, like many of his male peers, sees compliance as subsurvience—women either follow the rules or break them. Wow . . . that about says all that needs to be said about the challenge facing women in the workplace.

HIStory

MEN AT WORK today are the product of 2.5 million years of men at work in the past. Even though guys don't drag their knuckles on the ground anymore, *behavioral* evolution is notoriously slow. We all have prehistoric blood pumping through our twenty-first-century veins.

Let's go back a few million millennia. Even the name of the earliest-known species of man, *Homo habilis*, meaning "handy man," bespeaks what was most important for guys at the beginning of time. You got it: working, surviving, being handy with a tool. *Homo habili* who weren't handy with a club and a few sharp rocks not only perished, but decreased the likelihood of their families' survival as well. We're all descendants of the most capable of these handy guys. They were the strongest, most aggressive, smartest guys in the clan. All the other caveguys looked up to them. They had status. They wrestled wildebeests to the ground, outran saber-toothed tigers, fought Mother Nature, and survived long enough to have sex and procreate back home in the cave. The caveguys who couldn't cut it got buried.

Size mattered. Early males were much larger than females; their musculoskeletal systems were better equipped to outrun hungry bears. Pregnant females, or those with a toddler riding piggy back, might as well have worn an EAT ME sign on their backs. For the good of the clan, women stayed close to the cave while men competed with other men out on the veldt.

Fast-forward to 400 B.C. in ancient Greece, and it's a similar scenario. Men ran the government, worked the fields as slaves, spent a lot of time away from home with their cronies. Spartan boys were whisked away from their mothers at age seven and sent to military and athletic school for thirteen years. The *strong* boys, that is. Sickly babies were taken to the hills and left there to die of exposure. At school, Spartan boys traded the three Rs for the three Ts, Toughness, Tenacity, and Taking (pillaging doesn't have the same resonance, does it?)—a regimen that included inflicting and enduring serious pain—to improve their survival skills. They competed against one another, lived a no-frills barracks life with other soldiers, and basically learned how to be "manly" men.

The most respected manly men of ancient Greece trained for the Olympic Games. There, they could literally strut their manhood (they competed nude) in front of other men in an aggressive competition for the title of Alpha male ("alpha" being the first letter of the Greek alphabet). Greek women weren't even allowed to *watch* all those would-be gods dashing about in the buff. Not that they would have risked their femininity, anyway, since in ancient Greece, the ultimate sign of female beauty was a lily-white complexion. Think about it—what an ingenious way to keep women out of a man's business! The bright light of day literally sent Greek women running indoors, cementing the notion that a man's work was with men in the rough-and-tumble outside world while a woman belonged in the "protected" environment of the home.

See a pattern evolving here? Good, you've been paying attention.

About two thousand years later, on our own turf when the Pilgrims hit Plymouth Rock in 1620, a similar pattern took hold. Even though there weren't enough workers to build the New World and nearly every woman worked (it was considered a sin against God not to pitch in), men assumed all the power positions. Male Puritans and Separatists vigorously debated the future of the Colonies; men set up governments, established laws, owned and farmed land, and grew tobacco to use as "currency" in trade with Indians and with Europeans back home. Women were paid (by rich men, of course) to do essentially what they did so well at home: cook, clean, teach, weave, and midwife. Later, in 1692, women who showed independence, aggressiveness, or just unwillingness to go along with the "male" way were branded as witches and either hanged, pressed to death beneath heavy rocks, drowned, or burned at the stake. In those days, a woman with the audacity to question a powerful man (men were believed to be made in God's image; women were an afterthought) had to be possessed by the Devil. There was no other plausible explanation.

As our country expanded and agriculture took hold, men took charge of the land, competing for the most fertile fields, aggressively plowing, planting, tending, and harvesting before winter arrived. Again, size mattered. Men with the largest plantations were the most widely respected. Their families fared well; their seed lived on.

Competition, aggression, and status were the seeds of the Industrial Revolution as well. England, eager to maintain its competitive edge and keep its inventions to itself, wouldn't allow anyone who worked in a factory to leave the country. Crafty Americans stepped up to the plate and offered cash to anyone who could build a cotton-spinning machine in the United States. Money spoke louder than words. Apparently, a British factory worker named Samuel Slater snuck out of his country, crossed the Atlantic, and built a cotton-spinning machine from memory. Bingo. The Industrial Revolution landed on American soil.

Some of the biggest names in the Industrial Revolution were living, breathing examples of aggression and risk-taking. Charles Goodyear was a bankrupt hardware merchant when he walked into the country's first rubber company with a new valve he'd invented for rubber life preservers. His ideas were rejected and he ended up in debtor's prison, where he continued experimenting with rubber, though his family begged him to do something more sensible. John Deere took a huge risk by leaving his wife and family behind to join pioneers in Illinois who, he figured, might need a blacksmith. He was right. They also needed the steel plow he would ultimately invent and for which he'd become rich and famous. Robert Fulton, father of the steam engine, left home at age seventeen to make it as an artist in Philadelphia. He didn't. So at age thirty—middle-aged back then—he changed course, became an engineer, and changed history. These Alpha males of American capitalism were the role models for the Henry Fords, Louis B. Mayers, Ray Krocs, Ted Turners, and Bill Gateses to come.

With factories chugging along, the number of workers soared as quickly as the good ol' boy bosses entrenched themselves in power positions. Another sort of "pack mentality" took over: *unions*. Ordinary working men were able to unite and aggressively compete against the Alpha males who oppressed them.

The entire labor movement is a metaphor for the evolution of males at work. It became *collective* competition for power, unfortunately often excluding exploited women who had been hired as cheap labor to do jobs guys didn't want to do. As men fought for status, many women (even upper-class "distressed gentlewomen") had to scramble for jobs on their own, often accepting any "respectable" job available, meaning, of course, "women's work," the work of nannies, housekeepers, teachers, nurses. Most became seamstresses or, as they would soon be known, "slaves of the needle."

On July 13, 1848, a woman from Seneca Falls, New York, named Elizabeth Cady Stanton invited four female friends to tea. They all agreed that they were mad as hell with the plight of women and weren't going to take it lying down anymore. That afternoon, the women's rights movement was born. Life would never be the same for men again.

Women competing with men on *their* turf? This early women's movement ignited a primal fear as old as *Homo habilis*. Helping out was one thing—taking in laundry during the Depression to help feed the family, filling in for our boys overseas during the war by working in factories, taking a part-time job over the holidays to pay for extra gifts, teaching kindergarten kids, emptying bedpans, tidying up, running the sewing machine and the washing machine ('cause guys don't like to do that stuff)—but competing in the real cutthroat world, competing *against* guys, fathers, breadwinners, well, it was (and is) enough to rattle some men to their caveman core.

Men at Work

MEN HAUL historical baggage along with their attaché case, toolbox, or security clearance to work with them each day. A modern man's behavior at work is part caveman, part Greek god, part pioneer, part inventor, part organizer, part Superman. It's a product of evolution and socialization. Caveman left the cave each morning to slay beasts and bring home the bacon. Modern man gets into the 4×4 and battles the freeway.

Aggressive, fleet-footed Greek Olympians beat the competition and brought home the gold. Aggressive modern males are the Masters of the Universe, foremen, managers, supervisors who can afford to feed their families and give their kids a future.

Industrialists built empires and spawned large successful clans named Carnegie, Rockefeller, and Vanderbilt. Modern man notices that young nubile women are turned on by his wealth and big muscles and competence and the Armani suits he wears to the jungle each day. Competition feels sexy as long as he's winning. Aggression *works*.

Tim, thirty-eight, asked me why nice guys really do finish *last*. When I asked him to elaborate, he said that he'd been passed over for promotion twice in the past six months. "Both guys who got the jobs are widely considered arrogant, nasty SOBs. Do you think I have to change my nice-guy persona to ever get ahead at work?"

Well, Tim, *yes* and *no*. As every boss (even me) knows, having the buck stop at your desk isn't always fun or easy. Bosses have to be tough, make hard decisions, attract good people to work for the company, fire those who don't work out, keep an eye on the bottom line, and manage sometimes unmanageable personalities. Being "nice" rarely convinces the higher-ups that the prospect has the goods to do the job. Aggressive, dominating types more likely fit the bill. That said, there's a difference between aggressive behavior and spiteful, pompous, cruel conduct.

Where some guys go wrong at work is blurring that distinction. Where guys go right (to the top) is balancing dominance and aggression for the good of the company with consideration and respect for the good of their coworkers. I admit my major failing as a boss is a tendency to be too "nice," to not set clear enough limits, to be too undefined in terms of responsibilities. Then I get my feelings hurt when things don't work well. I'm being too much of a "girl" and not enough of a boss.

Working It Out Together

WHETHER YOU'RE a man or a woman, you're going to work with the opposite sex. Male-only bastions are gone. Women are even working their way into the priesthood. The days of women trying to "mimic" men at work are long gone, too. Remember the female *tie*—that humongous bow-*thang* peering out of a woman's serious suit? Ugh. The workplace is changing because women have been schooled in compromise, men in "all or nothing" and "conquer or submit." With all those females scurrying around searching for conciliation and cooperation, it's a lot slipperier trying to decide who's in charge of whom. The evolution of men and women working together is really a fine-tuning of the balance between his and hers, dominance and compromise, aggression and assertiveness, tradition and reality, and most of all denial and acceptance. Understanding and appreciating each other's biological, social, and emotional differences, and why men and women may lock horns at work, can help us *all* get ahead.

Jane, if you work for a guy, expect him to at least occasionally assert dominance over you. This may take the form of him towering over your desk, "barking" orders, treating you brusquely at times. The point here is not to take it personally. It's not about *you*, it's about his perceived place in the pecking order of the working world. You needn't cower beneath him. Certainly, you don't have to wear a perpetual KICK ME sign on your derriere. Attempts to one-up him or pull him down a peg will only backfire on you. Not a good idea. Understand that his behavior is a product of being a male in America. It was firmly in place before you ever entered the office . . . or maybe even the world. Focus on doing a good job. Period. If he demands more than you feel you ought to do, get a job description in writing. Take pleasure in your *paycheck*. Fill your need to be cherished and stroked after hours with a sympathetic friend, sensual lover, or cuddly pooch.

JUNGLE GEMS

Understanding men at work means accepting these basic male notions:

✦ *Work is war.*
✦ *War is competition.*
✦ *Men play all-or-nothing games.*
✦ *Competition is serious and fun . . . when you win.*
✦ *Winning is everything.*

And lookie here, Tarzan, if you work for a woman, pay attention to your behavior and feelings for a week. You may notice that you look for excuses to stand up when your boss sits down; you may show up a few minutes late for a meeting with her; you may bad-mouth her to others. You may feel both frustrated by her and attracted to her at times. These are all common reactions to male socialization in our culture. Though you may know better intellectually, emotionally you're dealing with feelings and behaviors that have been in place from the beginning of time. This doesn't give you permission to be insubordinate or disrespectful. Both are bad ideas and counterproductive. Instead, accept where you're at, appreciate the time, effort, and competence it took for your boss to get to where she's at, and shift your need to dominate and control onto specific tasks on the job. Compete with the challenges of your *work*, not the superiors who manage your work.

MALE AND FEMALE brains are wired differently. Male brains tend to process information in an either/or way. The corpus callosum, or the section of the brain that connects the right hemisphere to the left, is usually thinner in males. This means that men typically use one side of their brain to think and communicate, while women bounce back and forth between both sides. In guys, this produces quick, solution-oriented, linear thinking. You got a problem, I got a solution. Next! Guys tend not to see as many gray areas as women do. They focus on one black-and-white area at a time. Which also explains why so many men get annoyed at work when meetings seem to linger on. What's the point? they ask, exasperated. Let's get on with it.

Because male brain function makes it easier for men to focus on one thing at a time, men, in general, have more rigid lives. They divvy up their schedules: work time, self time, friend time, family time. There isn't a lot of overlapping. When guys are at work, they are *at work.*

I was once at a wedding reception in Los Angeles. A prominent TV movie producer was seated next to me. His wife was seated at the opposite curve of a huge round table. We got to chatting, and after a few sips of champagne, he confessed that he was frustrated with his wife because she didn't support his work. "A lot of the time, working means sitting at home reading scripts and books and watching what my competition is doing on television," he explained. "When my wife is home, she's making lunches for the kids, answering the phone, signing for FedEx packages. She wants me to help out, but how can I concentrate on my work with a million interruptions?"

Guys who work at home, particularly artists or freelancers, are hit with a double whammy. When they do what they are socialized to do—focus on work and succeed—they are often in a tug-of-war with the "jugglers" they married who can work *and* be a mom *and* manage the house *and* make scrumptious dinners in five minutes flat.

Ironically, later during that same wedding reception, the producer's wife and I had a similar conversation. Her take on the situation was slightly different. "My husband works twenty-four hours a day," she told me. "I can't reach him because even when he's home, he's always at work. What can I do?"

Both perspectives are quite accurate, though the situation is frustrating for both sides. Still, the solution is simple. I suggested that she schedule a weekly meeting with him. Book it, mark it on his calendar, keep it short and precise. Understand how important his work is to him, speak his language, and focus on what needs to be *done* rather than issue a general cry for "Help!" Allowing him to feel successful, instead of forever on the verge of disappointing his mate, will make *both* partners feel successful.

Look, Jane, forcing, nagging, cajoling, enticing, or manipulating him into being like you isn't going to work. And it's going to make you feel rotten and unappreciated to boot. He's not going to act or think or feel like you do because, *ta-da,* he's a GUY. Communicating to him in a language he understands is the best way to get what you want. For example, if you'd like him to call, instead of pointing out how childish and inconsiderate he is for *not* calling, tell him how you look forward to having your special time of day together. Ask him what would work best for him in terms of scheduling, and ask if he'd prefer that you check in with him, or he checks in with you because you realize he's busy and can get focused on something so intensely he loses track of time. All of us respond better to praise than pressure. Keep in mind he's *not* stupid and neither are you. Be direct. Ask specifically for what you want. Don't whine. Stick to the problem at hand and never, ever insult his mother.

If these techniques are important on the home front, where men and women have always attempted to work together—and they are—they're even more useful at work, which has only recently partnered men and women on a large scale. Understand that communication, body language, and a slew of biological, sociological, and psychological differences conspire to separate the sexes at work. Men network to build a power base. Women network to build relationships they can rely on later, if necessary. Female bosses often soften directives by asking subordinates to "do me a favor" or "if you have a minute, would you please. . . ." Male bosses tend to issue orders or ask specifically for what they want. Women worry about being respected, taken seriously. Men worry about embarrassing their families, about being an inadequate

Alpha male. They'll do almost anything to avoid looking foolish at work, where there's so much at stake.

Jane, don't be naive: Expect male coworkers to compete with you. It's what a guy has been programmed to do. Understand that it may not be enough for him to succeed—he may want you to fail, too. It's a waste of time to try to erase his competitive spirit at work. The most you can hope for is to channel his competitiveness into a team spirit thing that compels him to beat the other team rather than you. From his point of view, business is a blood sport. You may try going for a few throats yourself. Knowing that trying to soften him up is a losing game may inspire you to toughen up. There's nothing wrong with playing with the big boys as long as you understand that they are *always* out to win. Ties only count when they're worn around his neck.

Power struggles between men and women at work upset most men's deeply rooted socialization that boys don't beat up on girls, they *protect* them. Girls are sugar and spice, not barracudas in the boardroom. So when you're the boss, Jane, assume that there will be a skirmish or two over who's in charge. I'm not suggesting that men can't work for women. They can, and do quite successfully. It's likely, however, that he'll attempt a mini-coup or two. He may subconsciously feel it's his "manly" duty. What would the other animals think if he didn't? Again, don't take it personally. Just because he tries doesn't mean he'll succeed. Fight fang to fang, if necessary. Rise up as the Alpha female you are and he'll quickly recognize who's the boss. And be careful of flirtation. He may fall back on primitive behaviors and try to gain dominance sexually. It's never a good idea to fool around with someone at work, and it's *really* not a good idea to fool around with someone who works for you. Set an example of professionalism and insist that he follow suit.

One reason why sexual harassment can be such a polarizing issue between men and women is that we have yet to develop a unisex language to translate the legal definition of "unwelcome sexual advances, requests for sexual favors, and other verbal or physical conduct of a sexual nature that explicitly or implicitly affects an individual's employment, unreasonably interferes with an individual's work performance or creates an intimidating, hostile or offensive work environment."

What's "unreasonable"? Talking about a racy *Seinfeld* episode? Making a pass? Asking for a date? How do you know it's unwelcome unless you try? What's more offensive, telling a coworker she looks great in that sexy dress or asking if she'd like to have a drink with you after hours?

No doubt it's a confusing time to be a man. Or a woman. While men's behavior has evolved over millennia, in business, women's roles have changed radically in just the past few decades. It's been a revolution rather than an evolution. And when sociology butts up against psychology and biology, it dissolves everybody's good intentions. Understand that behavior is ultimately about *surviving*. Everybody behaves in ways that work for them, though not always consciously. Change—becoming more empathetic, less aggressive, more flexible, less fearful—is slow and difficult. Understanding and acceptance shorten the waiting period.

QUANTUM

MEN

Work two fewer hours a month and spend it talking to a woman you love who's not related by blood (come on, guys, that's thirty minutes a week—eat at your desk, already).

Ask yourself twice a year if your job is making you happy. Why or why not?

Ask yourself what you'd love to do.

Remember your happiest workday. Why was it happy?

Remember your worst workday. Why was it lousy?

WOMEN

Stop taking it personally when he spends time away from you.

Listen to what he wants to talk about.

Ask him what you can do for him today in public, not in the bedroom.

Work hard at something outside the home for forty hours next week.

Pay someone once to do what you hate most around the house.

LEAPS

Two

The Lair

Men at Home

A<small>T THE FIRST SIGN</small> of snow or cold weather, a male grizzly bear snuggles up in his rock cave or hollowed-out tree trunk and hibernates until spring. His normal heart rate of forty to seventy beats per minute drops to about eight to twelve beats. His metabolism slows by half. He doesn't even rouse himself to relieve himself. A bear's body can recycle urea into usable proteins all winter long. Male bears lie around in their lairs snoozing until warm weather wakes them up.

Female bears drift off into a drowsy, dormant state, too. Only their lairs are much more than just a place to crash for the winter. Female bears give *birth* while they hibernate. They feed their cubs. Their dens will help shelter and protect the cubs for this winter and the next.

At the end of a long day at work, a male human comes home to his lair, gives his wife and kids a bear hug, then plops down on the couch to hibernate for the night. Typically, his wife is getting dinner ready, keeping the kids quiet, and giving him some space. Which is exactly what he wants.

When guys come home from work, they want to be *anesthetized*. They've been worked up all day, so when they get home they want to feel safe. They don't want to be challenged, nagged, pestered, chattered at, saddled with the kids, given a To Do list, smothered, mothered, or bothered. For men, the workday is war. When they get home, they want peace.

Understanding why a man acts the way he does at home—in his lair—is understanding all about *turf*. Turf is about planting your feet where you belong, being *rooted*, secure, safe. Turf is territory. Both words originate from Latin words for earth, ground, peat, land, firm, and solid soil. Turf is not to be confused with the word *domain*, as in "The kitchen is a woman's domain." A domain is a sphere of influence; turf or territory connotes ownership. It's where a man is king of his castle, lord of the manor, lion of the den, bear of the lair. The notion that "it's *my* house, *my* woman, *my* kids, *my* responsibilities, *my* control" is so deeply ingrained in most guys' psyches that it persists even if a man co-owns his home with his wife, hires a nanny to raise the kids or leaves it entirely up to Mom, or marries a self-sufficient, independent woman and spends most of his time at work.

For a man, what happens under *his* roof is his business, his jurisdiction. Anything that superficially seems contradictory (when a woman acts as if it's *her* house, elderly parents move in and seem to take over, adult children come home, young kids disregard Dad, the dog obeys only Mom) will only *increase* his need to exert dominance. Guys want to feel that they are the ultimate authority in their lair. At home, a man needs to be master of all he surveys, especially if he doesn't feel that way at work.

Turf *marking* is one way men assert dominance at home. Males mark their turf much in the same way a dog squirts every fire hydrant in his neighborhood, elks rub their antlers on branches, or bears rub their scent onto a tree trunk. Men drop underwear on the bedroom floor and dirty socks outside the laundry hamper, leave newspapers strewn about the living room and change piled on the dresser and toilet seats up and plates behind on the table. The message these messes convey is "This is *my* space. I am man, hear me roar."

Animal markers indicate the sex of an animal, as well as its health, status, size, and readiness to mate. Human markers are signs of power and dominance. A true king of the castle needn't answer to anyone. Certainly, he needn't pick up after himself. And woe to the woman who tries to "mother" him into "good" or more civilized behavior.

Another way men assert dominance and define their turf is to designate "men's" work and "women's" work around the lair. Guys view barbecuing as "masculine," while baking or preparing the kids' lunches may be considered "feminine." Taming the fire in the fireplace is a man's job; making hot cocoa on the stove is woman's work. Mowing the lawn is a guy thing; vacuuming the rug is a girl thing. Even when guys do the dishes or the laundry or the grocery shopping or diaper the baby or other "feminine" chores, they often leave their *mark* by "forgetting" to wash one pot, or "accidentally" tossing a red T-shirt in the washing machine with the whites, or returning from the supermarket with everything but what you needed. Women often view this behavior as defiant or just plain lazy when, really, the men are just subconsciously declaring control over their turf—and expecting extravagant praise for helping out.

Elyse, forty-two, was at her wit's end when she called my radio program. Married twenty-one years, she said her husband,

Gene, "just didn't care" anymore. She said he discounted her, didn't appreciate her, and made her feel like his "servant." When I asked for a specific example, she told me about an argument they have several times a week. "I get up earlier than Gene does and make coffee for the two of us every morning," she said. "Gene stays up late. All I ask is that he refill the water purifier pitcher in the refrigerator before he goes to bed so I have enough water to make the coffee when I wake up. Simple, right? You'd think I was asking him to harvest fresh coffee beans."

Several times a week, Elyse wakes up to find the water pitcher empty and her anger in full bloom. "He doesn't care enough about me to do one simple thing," she lamented. While it's understandable that Elyse is frustrated, and her husband is probably exhibiting a passive/aggressive resistance to being told what to do, it's unlikely he is communicating anything about his feelings for *her* through the empty water pitcher. Women often assume that every action on a man's part is some sort of hidden message about his true feelings of love or lack of love for her, forgetting the psychological reality that most behavior reflects the wants and needs of the actor, not the audience.

Women mistakenly assume that men are constantly either taking the temperature of a relationship or sending signals about the current state of that relationship because that's what they, the women, do. Women have traditionally been the primary caretakers of infants—those wiggly little need machines who can't speak; they've been trained to scan behavior, facial expressions, sighs, whimpers, twitches for clues of discomfort or distress or delight. Babies' lives depend on it. But men are not babies. They *can* talk and walk and use sharp utensils on their own. Women needn't scan a man's behavior for hidden meaning; they need only ask him what's going on (and accept it when he says, "Nothing").

In other words, Jane, be willing to let it go or not take it quite so personally or deal with *your* feelings of anguish as completely dependent on how he is feeling or behaving. We can't always be clued in. Deal with it. In Elyse's case, Gene's behavior is probably not saying anything about his love, but he's saying a lot about his *turf.* He's communicating, "Even though you're telling me what to do, I'm still in charge. You're not my mom and you can't push me around."

The best way to deal with this type of territorial behavior is to, first of all, *understand* it. You mustn't take it personally. He's not taking a swipe at the closest female object. More likely, he's reacting to stresses at *work.* He can't lash out at anybody there—male or female. The risks are too great. We're talking primordial male animal instinct here. As Elyse and you and every other woman knows, nagging him won't work. Nagging makes men feel like little boys, and little boys are not lion kings. Making him feel like a little boy only guarantees that he'll dig his heels in harder to regain the status he feels he's lost.

What *does* work is allowing a man to feel as though his behavior in his lair is *his* choice. Make it worth his while. Make a deal with him. Each time he fills the water pitcher, empties the garbage, washes all the dishes, folds the laundry, picks the kids up at school, give him a voucher. He can save up his vouchers and redeem them for a night of wild sex or his mom's pot roast or a reprieve from housework for fifteen days. Ten vouchers means you give him a massage before you make love or eat dinner; twenty vouchers means you're his sex slave for the entire night or Julia Child for the week. Appeal to his animal nature and he'll respond to your human needs.

A few weeks ago I was out to dinner with friends when the conversation shifted to the definition of the "ideal" woman. When

JUNGLE GEMS

Understanding men at home means accepting these basic male notions:

✦ *Home is turf. Turf is to be marked, defined, and defended.*

✦ *Turf is about control and feeling safe.*

✦ *Feeling safe means feeling accepted, not criticized.*

✦ *A safe haven is a happy home.*

✦ *A man's home is his castle . . . but the vassals clean it.*

I asked one of the men, a guy in his mid-forties, whom he would choose as the perfect wife, he said without hesitation, "Sophia Loren." Okay, Oedipal undertones aside (she's sixty-four and busty!), he insisted it wasn't because she's beautiful, lusty, and, yeah, busty. "She's an amazing *cook,*" he said, adding that he'd read an article that said she'd insisted on having her own kitchen whenever she was on location and loved cooking for men. "Now, there's a great woman!" he said.

Deep down, guys feel as though the home should be maintained for them, their wife and kids should feed and pay homage to them. Period. Men don't willingly or easily do chores around the house because they feel they're not *manly.* That's what you're dealing with, Jane. And as for cooking, guys are willing to barbecue (it's *fire* and it's *outside)* or make something that gets lots of attention (salad or dessert or drinks), but cleanup, veggies, day-to-day drudgery . . . I don't think so—that's women's work! (Don't worry, it's not personal; it's testosterone.)

The truth you have to make clear is that housework isn't man's work or woman's work. It's *house*work. And since you're both living there, then you both should be doing it. But if both spouses work outside the home, maybe hiring someone to work *inside* the home will short-circuit a lot of arguments and give both partners what they really want at home: peace.

Animal Instincts

N THE ANIMAL world, the battle to define and defend turf is ongoing. Male wapiti elks spend their entire day fighting off other male intruders and rounding up wayward does who venture beyond their territorial limits. While both males and females mark territories, males typically set the limits as to where *their* females can roam. Keeping an eye on them at all times is the only way they can make sure the offspring are really theirs. Even when female animals create their own lairs, they tend to stick close to home, giving themselves far less space to roam than their male partners do.

The brown bear is a perfect example of how male and female definitions of territory differ. The adult male's "home range" is usually four to six times larger than the female's. Female bears create a safe area close to the den and food sources. Male bears roam about more freely. In fact, the territory of the mature male bear overlaps into that of *several* other females. Guy bears feel at home nosing around other females, mating as often as possible. (Bears are solitary creatures; when they encounter one another, they make the most of it.) Female bears feel most at home with the cubs.

Human males often see nothing wrong with nosing around other females when they are away from home, either. Many men don't consider extramarital sex to be adultery if they are two hundred miles or more away from home. It's no accident that prostitution is alive and kicking at conventions. Again, it's a territorial thing. Guys expand their territories to include wherever they are, whatever they perceive they own—their car, their garage, the lodge on Monday nights. Get in the car with a guy at the wheel and you'll see male territorialism in action: The road is his battleground, his lane is his turf, other drivers are competitors, his horn is his roar.

Yet even human male animals want their females to respect the narrow boundaries they have marked for them near the home base. That's why guys usually drive on a road trip and women aren't welcome at the Elks Club. That's why infidelity is so much more destructive to a marriage when the *woman* cheats. She's not only violated her wedding vows, she's invited a competitor onto her husband's turf—even if the affair happens in a hotel or another location, *she's* his territory and her betrayal has sullied his empire, diminished his status, and rendered him weak.

Of course, if the affair does happen at home, it's the ultimate stab in the back. It means his wife is out of control. And a man who can't control his woman is a man who can't control his turf. Which means he's lost status, he's vulnerable to attack, he can't protect his family or his territory, and the whole kingdom knows it. Soon the vultures will be circling.

Charlotte, twenty-six, wrote me that she was stunned that her husband of five years wanted a divorce. She sorrowfully related that he'd been cheating on *her* their whole married life. "I even caught him red-handed once," she wrote. He was away on business, she popped up to surprise him, and the surprise was on her. "I was devastated, but he apologized and begged for forgiveness and promised it would never happen again. I wanted our marriage to work so badly, I willed myself to look the other way."

While she was looking the other way, Charlotte's husband had several other liaisons. Eventually she was so hurt and angry and so wanted revenge that she initiated a brief affair with her husband's cousin. (Charlotte, let's not play dumb . . . his *cousin*, for heaven's sake. Talk about maximum embarrassment.) She clearly wanted her husband to find out so he'd feel the same pain she'd felt for the past five years.

He did. "It was awful. He looked like I'd driven a butcher knife through his heart. The following week he filed for divorce." Charlotte was flabbergasted and completely taken aback by his vehemence. No matter how hard she pled for mercy, her husband was adamant. "He told me he could never forgive me for messing with his family."

Charlotte defiled her husband's turf. She humiliated him in front of his clan, other male competitors. Though he'd done the same to her, in his mind there was no comparison. And no repairing the damage, either.

WILD THINGS

Q. *When it comes to an animal's territory:*
  a. Bigger is better.
  b. Location, location, location.
  c. Just enough is just right.

A. *Just enough is just right.* Unlike many humans, animals are not into conspicuous consumption. It's not about having the biggest turf, but the easiest to defend. A wild animal's territory rarely extends beyond the boundaries of exactly what he needs to feed himself and his family or his harem and breed successfully. While location is important, it's almost always centered around the best location for food. The rest can be worked out. Interestingly, the human desire to acquire *stuff* and live in the biggest house on the block and drive the largest SUV actually puts us at greater risk of predators. It goes against our animal natures to keep it simple.

Q. *If the adult grouse loses his territory, he:*
    a. Loses the will to live
    b. Stalks another grouse until he can overtake *his* turf
    c. Attempts to mate with another male's female so he can "inherit" his territory

A. *Loses the will to live.* Territory is so important to an animal's sense of security that the round, plump game bird—the grouse—often withers up and dies if younger, stronger birds evict him from his turf. In the animal world, familiarity doesn't breed contempt; familiarity creates the safe haven animals need in order to thrive and breed. Similarly, aging humans who are removed from their familiar surroundings and taken to live in a nursing home, for instance, often lose the desire to get up, get out of bed, and get on with life.

Q. *Nesting instincts are solely the dominion of the female animal.*
    a. True
    b. False

A. *False.* Some male animals, such as Australia's bowerbird, are so attached to their nests, they create elaborate homes. The bowerbird's nest is an intricate, vertical structure, sometimes as tall as seven feet. He decorates it with leaves and feathers and maybe a bottle cap or two he finds on the ground. The major difference between male nest-building and female nest-building is where nature, again, takes its course. Males build elaborate nests to attract a mate (or two). Females nest to protect and feed their offspring. The human male uses his bachelor pad lair complete with brown velvet king-sized water bed to entice his girlfriend, and bingo, she wants to redo the kitchen.

Boys to Men

HUMAN MALE turf-building begins in childhood. Boys build forts, tree houses with NO TRESPASSING signs, pup tents in the backyard for sleepovers that feel as if they're miles from home instead of steps from Mom and Dad's back door. Watch little boys play and listen for the word that keeps popping up: *mine*. As soon as boys are old enough to define themselves as separate from their parents, they start carving out their own territory and designating its inhabitants—*my* truck, *my* book, *my* pajamas, *my* bunk in the bunk bed.

Girl babies of the same age behave the same, but as females get older, there is more emphasis on sharing: Barbies, secrets, clothes, time. As males get older, their "turf" becomes their position in line in the school cafeteria, a favorite seat on the bus, their bedroom with the KEEP OUT sign posted on the shut door. Whenever boys are in a line together or a group, they're jostling, elbowing, poking, and prodding one another. This behavior is their fledgling attempt to mark and defend territorial boundaries.

The whole notion of sharing goes against a boy's instinctual grain. Sharing invites competitors onto their turf and feels threat-

ening. Henry, a forty-eight-year-old father of three (who was one
of *seven* kids), called about a child-rearing dispute he was having
with his wife, Melissa (an only child). "Melissa insisted the kids,
just a year apart, share all their toys with each other. Our
Hanukkah celebration each year ended in a pile of communal gifts
that everybody fought over. I wanted my kids to have their *own*
presents, their *own* rooms, their *own* separate lives—like I wasn't
allowed to have when I was a kid."

　　I suggested to Henry that this wasn't a battle over the vir-
tue of sharing, but a turf war—between him and his wife, and one
created by them between their kids. Melissa never needed to flex
any territorial muscles when she was a kid because her parents,
her Barbie doll, her pink canopy bed were all *hers*. She probably longed to share her territory with a sibling because she never
had to.

　　Henry admitted that part of the problem for him was that as
a child he was "forced" to share a room with his younger brother
until he left home for college. To him, sharing meant *losing*—
privacy, independence, status, peace. Sharing felt uncomfortable.
Melissa viewed sharing only as *gaining*—companionship, love,
freedom from loneliness. Sharing felt pleasurable. Instead of letting their kids feel their own sense of ownership before they gave
it away to their siblings, Melissa forced the issue. Understanding
what sharing really means to her husband and her kids allowed
Melissa to step back a bit and let her children sort it out on their
own while she sorted it out with their dad.

HIStory

<hr>

MALE TERRITORIALISM IS as old as time. From the first nomadic Natufian tribe in western Asia whose existence was defined by their constant search for the best place to hunt and house their families, to the Persian Sassanid king Ardashir I, who defeated the last Parthian king, Artabanas V, in 224 A.D., to the raiders from Denmark and Norway who initiated the Viking Age, guys have been procuring and protecting their turf throughout history. Warriors were considered the manliest of men.

Take Alexander the Great. In 336 B.C., at the virile age of twenty, he became king of Macedonia. At twenty-two, he was itching for more, so he conquered the Greek portion of the Achaemenid Empire to become king of Greece. He then went on to secure most of Egypt. After consulting the Oracle at Delphi, who told him, "Thou art invincible, my son" (Where can you find a good oracle when you need one these days?), Alexander invaded Persia and India and would have kept going if he hadn't dropped dead of exhaustion at the ripe old age of thirty-two. He was hailed as heroic, powerful, seductive, and, according to the Oracle, invincible. What guy doesn't want to be invincible? What woman isn't attracted to a sexy, invincible conqueror? Look, if manly brawn and sweat and conquest weren't sexy, Alexander would probably be remembered as Alexander the Raging Lunatic instead of Alexander the Great.

The point is, turf battles are as male as five o'clock shadow. And when guys don't have a kingdom to conquer, they'll transfer their territorialism to the kingdom within their own property limits, controlling everything that happens on their land or in their homes. Historically, men had every legal right to treat their land, as well as their women and children, as their sole property. Early Roman law decreed women and children as forever inferior to men. In medieval marriages, the husband had the right to beat his wife as long as he didn't kill her. Peasant widows in medieval England were forced to pay a death tax to their husband's liege lord that typically consisted of the family's best animal, regardless of the economic hardship imposed on his survivors. Under England's common law, any married woman gave up her name and virtually all her property to her husband's control.

Democratic institutions aside, during the early years of the United States, a man essentially legally owned his wife and kids, even maintaining legal control of the kids and the property in the event of a divorce. The sociological roots for female subservience run deep. Even today, several cultures, such as Islamic, Hasidic, and in some cases Latin, view women as belonging in the home with the kids. Period.

Ironically, though men historically dubbed women the "weaker" sex, early housework was grueling, heavy, hard, backbreaking labor. In pioneer America, for instance, water had to be hauled daily from streams to wash clothes by hand by stirring them in large pots on the hearth, wringing them dry, and hanging them outside. Soap and candles were handmade from rendered animal fat. Clothes, sheets, curtains, and towels were spun from sheep's wool or made from animal skins. Heavy irons heated on the stove were used to press clothing. Dirt floors had to be swept daily. Chickens were killed and plucked, gardens were tilled and harvested, children were bathed and fed and raised. The life of a housewife was anything but gentle . . . for *centuries.* Cleaning detergents weren't even produced in the United States until the 1930s. Women swept every inch of their rugs with *brooms* each day. The vacuum cleaner wasn't invented until 1907, and the first

Hoover weighed twenty-five pounds. Women were on their hands and knees so much they wore aprons with built-in knee pads.

I'm not suggesting that men working the fields and the factories didn't do hard labor. They certainly did. However, the notion of men coddling and protecting their women from the harsh outside world by keeping them safely and serenely on the home turf was true only for the upper classes. The reality is, women historically accepted their position in the family for *economic* reasons. Until recently, marriage was largely an economic vehicle to allow for the care and feeding of dependent women and children. Many women simply couldn't survive without men to support them financially. They accepted their lot since there was precious little alternative legally, financially, or societally. That's why turf battles at home between men and women didn't really kick in until women entered the workforce.

Men at Home

WHEN A MAN puts his key in the lock of his front door—whether it's the door to a trailer, a tract house in the 'burbs, an estate in the country, a boat, or a tree house—he's dealing with ancient history as well as modern reality. Emotionally he wants his woman and children to pay homage to the arrival of the king. At the very least, he wants his minions to give him some peace and quiet while they scuttle off to make his meal and fluff his pillow for the night.

Realistically, men understand that their women have had a hard day, too. They want to listen and be supportive. They want to fix whatever is bothering her, make her problems go away. But a man knows he can't control his woman's work environment or her feelings, so he's stuck. His whole being wants to protect her, but he knows he can't. This is the struggle. A modern male at home struggles between the forces of his nature, his desire to be nurtured and his need to protect. Often this internal battle results in a weary warrior plopped down on the couch in front of the tube, his wife angry and resentful and feeling used. She attacks, he retreats, and his lair—supposedly his refuge from the jungle—is tense and uncomfortable and about as safe and welcoming as a snake pit.

Yvonne, thirty-seven, called my radio program with just this familiar complaint. "He works all day," she told me, "but I work all day and night." It's the *second shift* so many women have come to know. Their shift as mother and housewife begins the moment they get home from work. "I told my husband if he didn't help me more, I was going to ask my mother to live with us. It's not the ideal solution, I know, but I'm at the end of my rope."

Yvonne's husband was apparently at the end of his rope, too. "He flipped out," she said. "He told me if my mother moved in, he was moving out. Then he stormed out of the house and didn't come back until late that night. The next day, it was like nothing had happened. I came home from work, started making dinner, helped the kids with the homework. He turned on the CD player and crashed on the couch. We're right back where we started."

Ultimatums don't work. As Yvonne found out, threats just send men packing. Especially in his lair—his safe haven where he needs to maintain control—ultimatums are a flashing red light: *Danger Ahead!* Yvonne only ignited her husband's fight-or-flight response. In this case, he took off. Other guys might have stood their ground and lashed out instead. Either way, Yvonne didn't get what she wanted—a little help around the house.

A more productive way to handle the situation would be to get a sitter, ask your husband out on a date, get out of the house, and have a romantic candlelit dinner. Say, "I love spending time with you. Let's figure out a way to have more free time together." Then let him mull it over. Give him the time and space to do what he is genetically, sociologically, psychologically, and culturally programmed to do: protect his mate, create peace in his lair, feel powerful, take charge, and—if all works out—get his wife into bed.

Change, change, change.

I'm not suggesting that women revert to the fifties model or retreat to some female mystique thing. Letting the man make all the decisions, arriving home early from work to get the kids bathed and quiet and the roast in the oven and fresh lipstick on, is ludicrous in today's world. What I am suggesting is that we women make it possible for each of us to make the other feel *cherished.* It's the basis of a loving relationship. This means women understanding that men often arrive home feeling as if they've spent the day as an ox pulling a plow. And likewise men must understand that women often feel like worker bees—buzzing about tending to everyone's needs—when, just once, they'd like to feel like the queen.

So, Jane, understand that the ancient notion of "ownership," or "You are *my* woman," is likely to creep up out of nowhere from time to time. He may even be surprised to feel proprietary toward you. But history dies hard in the soul of man. His subconscious may be telling him, "She's *my* woman. She should do what *I* say in *my* home." Fighting his subconscious is a losing battle. Accept who he is at this moment and don't take it personally. His innate need to feel powerful and in control is as strong as your need to feel independent and cherished. Neither one is right or wrong, it's just what *is.* You know your husband. You know what turns him on. If you want him to help you around the house, figure out how to make it worth his while. Bribery is a perfectly good motivator. It's the fine art of helping someone understand what's in it for him if he does what you want him to do. It's not manipulative; you're merely working with his nature and your nature to *nurture* a happy marriage.

And, Jane, now that you're working outside the home just as hard as your husband does, you've probably adopted many traditionally "male" feelings about the lair. You need to chill out after a hard day, too. Let your husband know that you need some TLC, too. Instead of feeling like an adversary, or someone from a different planet, he'll likely understand this more readily than you might imagine. Your feeling what he feels makes for a powerful connection between the two of you. You can help *each other* by being very clear about what you need at home.

Tarzan, let's deal with your issues for a moment. I understand that it's a confusing, frustrating time to be a man. You're out there struggling to be an Alpha male in the workplace and the dominant lion in your lair. You come home for a little tender, loving care, and your wife says you treat her like a scullery maid. I hear you. The rules have changed, and you may not be all that crazy about them. It's okay to feel that way, but guys who roar a lot at home and act like the king of beasts will probably end up living in the lair alone. You don't want that!

If you need a half hour to veg out, tell your wife. If you want to watch an uninterrupted football game on Sunday, tell her. You're not asking permission; you're avoiding a miscommunication that could ruin the evening or, in the latter case, the entire day on Sunday. Listen when she tells you what she needs, and negotiate a compromise just as you would at the office. It's not hard and you know how to do it.

Jane, what you must make clear to your Tarzan is that you understand that it's a confusing, frustrating time to be a man. He's out there struggling to be an Alpha male in the workplace and the dominant lion in your lair. He comes home for a little tender, loving care, and you say he treats you like a scullery maid. Let him know that you hear him. You understand that the rules have changed, and he may not be all that crazy about them. Tell him it's okay to feel that way, but that guys who roar a lot at home and act like the king of beasts will probably end up living in the lair alone. Neither of you wants that. Let him know that if he needs a half hour to veg out, he just needs to tell you. And if he wants to watch an uninterrupted football game on Sunday, to tell you so. You're not his mother. And he's not asking permission. What has to happen is that you both avoid the kind of miscommunication that can ruin an evening or an entire Sunday. If you can get him to listen, the two of you can negotiate a compromise just as you would at work. You give a little, he gives a little, and you meet in the middle (near the kitchen garbage can, which probably needs to be emptied!).

Working It Out Together

BATTLES ON THE home front can be resolved with a little understanding and a lot of dealing with specific situations rather than global complaints. Saying "I'll fix you dinner if my fanny doesn't hit water at three A.M. 'cause you've left the seat up" is much more effective than "You're an inconsiderate, thoughtless brute."

Jane, expect him to have a different standard of "clean" than
you do. Some guys are meticulous, but lots more are not. Your nesting urges will probably butt up against his "king of the castle"
needs at some point. That's okay. Men and women don't have to be
the same to get along. It's helpful, however, to *specifically* outline
what each partner is responsible for around the lair. And no detail
is too specific. If it's his job to empty the garbage, don't expect him
to empty it each time it's full. A guy's definition of "full" may be
when you can't cram one more Q-Tip into it. A woman's definition
may be the moment she throws away the cellophane that wrapped
the fish she's cooking for dinner. Often, men and women skirmish
about housework because they expect the other to think and feel
the way they do. Big mistake—and one that can easily be avoided by
taking the time to work out definitions that satisfy both of you.

Men are likely to come home feeling a bit beaten up by the
jungle of the workplace. Even when men enjoy their jobs, which a
lot of men do, the pressure they put on themselves, the pressure
women put on them, the pressure their bosses, friends, kids, parents, culture lay on their shoulders is enormous. Failing at work
means failing at *manhood* for most guys. Successful men are the
Alpha males in American society. The drive to be top dog is heavy
and often burdensome. When a man comes home, he wants his
burden *lifted,* not added to.

Men need a "coming down" period from the stress of the
workday. That's why happy hour was invented—initially it was a
time for guys to unwind before they had to rev up again to face the
pressures of family life. Schedule your own "happy hour"/let
down/relaxation/reemerge time at home with or without your presence, depending on his mood and preference. Alcohol needn't be a
part of it. The at-home happy hour is a scheduled span of relaxation
time (it doesn't have to be a whole hour), a sort of holding pattern

between the jungle and the lair. Arrange with the kids ahead of time that this is Dad's "time-out" and he's not to be interrupted. Allot a private space in the house (his *den,* perhaps?) and keep out without a specific invite in (without pouting!). No trespassing. For fifteen or twenty minutes each night, this is his fort, his tree house, his pup tent in the backyard.

Secondly, accept that men need to feel safe in their lairs. I'm not talking about bolt locks and sophisticated security systems, I'm talking about *emotional* safety. One of the most threatening things a woman can say is "We need to talk" the minute a man comes home. Guys hear, "Fire! Head for the exit!" They panic. Instantly, their animal instincts take over and they run, bare their fangs, or rise up and pound their chests, hoping to scare the intruder off. It's okay for women to have stuff they need to discuss with their man, but it's not okay to ambush him with it, which is how men view a woman's request to "talk." Instead, let him have his "happy hour," then schedule a meeting for later by casually saying, "There are a couple of things I want to work out when we can both give them fifteen minutes of undivided attention."

Make sure you put a time limit on it. Men instantly feel emotional claustrophobia at the thought of an endless "relation-ship" meeting in a closed room. Letting him know that it will be over soon is wildly reassuring. Better still, schedule a walk, a lunch date, a drive. Getting him off his turf will reduce his need to defend what he may view as an "attack."

Third, always separate housework and child-care issues. Taking care of the kids is not the same as doing the laundry; it's not fair to bury all household duties under one blanket phrase like "I do everything around here!" If you need help with the kids, ask for it. If you need help around the house, ask for it or hire it. And never, I repeat, *never,* hold off punishing the kids "until Father gets home." Making him the bad guy not only pits one parent against the other, it sends kids the message that Dad is strong and Mom is weak. Not a good idea.

Finally, understand that every living thing—men, women, kids, dogs, gorillas in the mist—move toward pleasure and away from pain. Men at home are no different. If women want men to happily help around the house, they need to make it more pleasurable for them. I'm not suggesting that women dust in the nude (hey, whatever works), but be creative. Giving guys a way of doing housework that's in their best interest is in the whole family's best interest, too. That means accepting that he may not clean as well as you do, praising what he does instead of criticizing what he doesn't do, offering enticing bribes, and lightening up a little. I've yet to meet a man who apologizes for the state of his messy apartment, but I've met tons of women who apologize for having one magazine out of alignment on the coffee table.

Jane, understanding what his turf, his *lair,* means to him is crucial. Being critical isn't necessary, or wise. Acceptance is the first step. All human animals are products of their genetics, upbringing, culture, history, peer influences, brains, bodies, and feelings. All this baggage is a heavy load, but one that can be lightened considerably by working within these limits, instead of butting up against the barriers. Trying to change your partner doesn't work; understanding him or her does.

QUANTUM

MEN

Meet her
more than halfway.

Tell her a
childhood memory.

Tell her a dream.

Pick up after yourself
for three days.

Put the toilet
seat down.

WOMEN

Tell him something you
love about him.

Defer one criticism for
one week.

Meet him halfway.

Leave his stuff where
it is; don't touch it, but
don't bitch.

Buy a rubber stamp with
your name on it.

LEAPS

Three

The Pride

Men and Their Kids

W HEN WE THINK "male lion," we think King of the Jungle, master of all he surveys, the MGM icon. The reality is much more mundane. The male lion loafs about the veldt, a prized stud who knows that all he has to do is look big, muscular, and gorgeous, and roar now and then. His females will kill for him, mate with him, and care for his energetic, curious, playful offspring so he can get his rest. This is still the animal kingdom, so even though lionesses do all the work, there's no question who's head of the household. A male lion struts about, easily asserting dominance with a tousle of his studly mane and a flash of sharp teeth.

Human male "cats" are heads of their households, too. They command respect at the dinner table, dole out the dough, assert dominance with a mighty roar now and then. They carry photos of their pride and joy in their wallets. Their wives stop by the supermarket on the way home from work, make dinner, care for the kids. Men "help out," but still do (at most) only half as much housework as women do. Hey, what's *kingly* about vacuuming or scrubbing a toilet? It's much more fun to stride through the jungle while the wife makes everything nice, neat, and quiet in the den so he can bask in the sun at the end of the day.

Understanding about men and their prides (hmm, interesting word, yes?)—their families—is understanding about the very notion of *pride* itself, of manhood, fatherhood, boyhood, and everything that goes into being a male. This chapter will show how modern fatherhood is a battle between nature, nurture, expectation, and political correctness. A man's family—his offspring—demonstrates to the world at large the male's ability to attract, impregnate, and keep a female. The veneer of a well-tailored business suit or a pair of tight jeans (ahem . . .) is window dressing to the basic underlying XY notion: "I am male, I've got a penis, I know how to use it."

The pride is where fathers teach their sons how to be "men." A man's family is a status symbol. His kids are his "little deductions," his wife is his "trophy." Imagine a woman boasting that her studly second spouse is a "trophy husband." Majorly unlikely. Men don't get as many face-lifts; they get Viagra. Youthful looks don't make men feel as powerful as performing well sexually. And nothing proves that a man can perform sexually more than the birth of his offspring.

When it comes to their families, men feel *proprietary*; women feel protective. Men feel a sense of ownership regarding their offspring. Even if they have little to do with raising their children, they take personal pride in their children's achievements. Listen to a man talk about his kids. He'll brag, "My son is going to Harvard" or "My daughter just got into med school" or "My boy made the varsity swim team." Mothers swell with pride, too, but they often talk of their child's "happiness" or how their *child* feels about attaining some goal: "Johnny is thrilled he was accepted to such a good school." Or they'll talk about their daughter's dating a doctor or an architect. It may not be politically correct, but men boast about the destination; women focus on the journey.

A man's family is an extension of himself—genetically, psychologically, legally, financially, and socially. His family—his pride —influences his standing in the community. The word *pride* derives from similar roots as the word *improve*—something useful, profitable, advantageous to have and hold. Think about it, when's the last time a *single* man ran for president? Candidates kiss *babies*, not women (well, at least until elected). A man with a family can be trusted, he's not a sexual predator (at least he's not perceived as one), he's not homosexual, he's not afraid of commitment, he's stable, he's a good provider. These are the attributes our society values in men—and statesmen.

JUNGLE GEMS

Understanding men and their families means accepting these basic male notions:

+ *Men raise their kids the way they were raised.*
+ *Men are raised to be aggressive and dominant.*
+ *Aggression and dominance work well on the job, not so well at home.*
+ *Home is turf.*
+ *Turf is about control.*
+ *Being nurturing and "soft" at home can feel scary and make a man feel out of control.*

Fathers often feel personally judged by the way their kids turn out, particularly their sons. A son's failure is a genetic black mark, a blight on the family name. Mothers tend to react to a wayward child with disappointment; fathers react in shame—their pride, quite literally, has been wounded.

Animal Instincts

T HE MALE EMPEROR penguin incubates the egg of his off-spring all winter long until his mate returns, with food, just in time to see her baby hatch. It's one of the few instances in the animal world where the father takes such an active role in caring for the young (although Mom takes over as soon as she gets back). Penguin dads take on baby duty for one evolution-ary reason—the female has more body fat and can survive the harsh winter weather while she searches for food better than the male. The penguin dad's job, balancing the egg on his feet and keeping it warm with his sagging belly, may be reflected in the human male keeping one eye on the kid playing Nintendo and one eye on the NFL play-offs. Phylogenetically—the way the species develops—both animal and human dads would probably rather leave all that baby stuff up to Mom, but a man's gotta do what a man's gotta do sometimes. Which is the way it is in almost every corner of the animal world. But the rest of the time, most ani-mals—including humans—leave the baby stuff up to Mom. 'Cause that's the way it's always been.

Biologically, of course, there's a reason why the mother/child bond is necessarily tight. Hey, Mom is where the milk is, she's where *life* is. Often, in the predator-eat-prey animal kingdom, this is where much of the danger is, too. Drooling carnivores look for young, inexperienced animals to stray from their protective mothers. Animal moms have a lot on their plates. Not only do they have to hunt or forage for the food to feed their young, they have to make sure their young don't get hunted themselves.

Male animals protect their young, too, but mostly they make sure other males don't get close enough to have sex with their women. Male animals spend their days protecting their status in the pride, which means keeping younger, stronger studs away from the baby-makers. In fact, when a younger, stronger male lion *does* force an older, weaker male away from his pride, the first thing he does as new lion "king" is kill all the small cubs in the pride. As savage as this sounds, it's more than just a "step"-lion feeling jealous of another male's cubs. By killing the female's young, the new Alpha causes the lionesses to become fertile again and ready to start a new pride with him.

This sense of ownership, translated into human terms, is similar to the stepfather who overdisciplines his wife's children or insists that he and his wife start a family "of their own" as soon as possible. It's part of the male animal nature to do what he can to make sure offspring are his and his alone. It's a *status* thing. Human males don't want younger, stronger studs muscling their way into their homes, their beds, seducing their baby-makers. Men with family status are those who have solid families for whom they provide solidly—by *working*, that is, bringing home a paycheck. It *doesn't* mean being Mr. Mom. The whole notion of men in our current culture being respected as househusbands is a bit of a joke. John Lennon got away with it only because he was a Beatle and had made tons of money. A man is still deemed only as potent as his paycheck. Look at Aristotle Onassis or Bill Gates or Prince Charles. Wealthy men get the women. It doesn't make any difference whether they are smart, attractive, sexy—they morph into all those things as soon as they make the big bucks.

Hey, before you women throw up your hands and ask whose side I'm on, or you guys decide no dirty diapers will ever have *your* name on them, chill. Men may absolutely *not* relinquish the idea that they can raise kids. Until men contribute substantially more time and energy to molding—not scolding—their offspring, society cannot progress. But the widespread acceptance of a new standard of male behavior is going to take some time (even God figured the Israelites needed forty years in the desert to change their thinking, and that was *God!*). Changing from King of the Roost to equal partner is no simple task, especially when it involves spit-up and poop.

Stay-at-home dads aren't the goal any more than stay-at-home moms are. The idea that *both* parents are *equally* responsible (but not in identical ways) for raising strong, self-reliant, happy kids is what it's all about.

What this means is this: Human male animals are genetically, psychologically, anthropologically, and evolutionarily programmed *not* to bring up baby. Nature *and* nurture conspire against men developing the intimacy, patience, attention, selflessness, and mindfulness it takes to rear needy kids. Men *are* wired to leave the cave and sally forth to collect whatever it takes to feed, clothe, and house baby. That would be fine, and the end of the story, if the rest of the world hadn't evolved beyond the Stone Age, or at least 1950, but we have. It's a braver new world out there with each passing year. Men and women both need to readjust the notion of what it takes to raise a *pride* we can all be proud of. And the first adjustment is that we have to ignore the way we're wired and start having real two-parent families—families where both parents are deeply involved in raising the kids.

Economically and emotionally, we now understand that all God's children need to feel important (even women), and work is one way to feel important. The idea of women working outside the home seems logical and understandable. Even more important, if women want their men to share child-rearing responsibilities, they *must* be willing to partially shoulder the financial burden. It really is a jungle out there; it's not fair to make men carry the whole load. Once women are willing to assume a share of the financial responsibility, the focus at home isn't on cleaning floors but molding their children's minds. Dusty bookshelves aren't important when your self-worth comes as much from the world beyond the front door as behind it.

The first thing men must do to overcome evolution is schedule time with their kids. Listen up, Tarzan: *Raising,* not only *having,* children is one of the most important things you'll ever do in your life. Understand that the term *provider* means providing love, time, attention, and affection as well as financial support. It's okay to want to succeed at work and give your family a good material life—it's admirable—but giving of your *self* is the best gift to them and for you.

Both of you have to understand that coparenting is the art of compromise. Figuring out how both parents can raise the kids takes a lot of creativity, problem-solving, and, yeah, *compromise.* Again, both parents must work. Unless you've won the lottery or inherited a fortune, sharing the financial onus of raising kids is as important as sharing car-pool duty. It's part of the deal. It comes with the territory. Sharing parental responsibilities with your wife is crucial if you want your kids to be well-rounded, loving individ-

uals, capable of loving themselves as much as you love them. By
"responsibilities" I don't just mean stuff you *do* with and for your
kids for an express purpose. Being a good parent also means just
being there, hanging out, sometimes. Consistency breeds security.
There's no substitute for *time.*

When we talk about parenting, we're talking about time allocation. The politics of family is time and resource allocation. Men
need to transfer some of their business skills onto their families. If
your kid were your boss, would you miss a meeting? Well, a concert
or a ball game or even a regular talk about what kind of day your kid
had is as important as any meeting, Tarzan. Why should the words
mom and *dad* mean such vastly different things? The answer is,
they shouldn't, even though they do.

Look, the only shot any of us ever have at reasonable emotional, sexual, romantic lives as adults is to be raised by both men
and women. Fewer and fewer kids are having any contact with
men. When they do, it's often superficial, judicial, punitive, or in
sixty-second increments between television segments. Fathers
often feel allowed to hug their sons only when they do well in
sports, not in life. It's taking a huge toll on all of us. Several sources
show that children from a fatherless home are twenty times more
likely to end up in prison, nine times more likely to drop out of
high school, ten times more likely to abuse chemical substances,
and, if a boy, fourteen times more likely to commit rape. And the
most likely group to be chronically poor are families with no
active, involved, supportive father.

Clearly, society is inadvertently moving in that direction of
necessity, with women assuming more financial burdens. Nurturing, hands-on dads are beginning to be "in." In a more balanced
world, fathers will routinely tote their kids to work, to day care, to
the pediatrician. They tuck them in at night and read them bed-

time stories. They will put Flintstones Band-Aids on their boo-boos when they fall. Sitcoms have led the way by taking the pipe and slippers out of Dad's hand and putting a diaper in it. Family time is beginning to increase. People work half days on Friday in the summer. White-collar workers work in their homes. Several companies offer "paternity" leave. The computer, fax, and modem are already changing the way that we work, and they have the potential to change parenting just as dramatically. But real change can't happen until we decide that our children are as important as work. And children won't be as important as work until women take some of the financial responsibility off men.

When the family can't get by without the man out there in the working world pounding his chest and doing the Alpha male thing, a woman can't say to her husband, "I need you to help raise the kids." The only thing he can say in reply is "If I do, we just won't make it." It's as simple as that.

Perhaps the answer is that both men and women should commit to their kids long before they arrive. Marry later, work longer hours before the kids are born, save money, take time off work when the kids *do* arrive, and commit to a family plan of *raising* kids together, not just *having* kids together. The notion of "quality" time is ridiculous; kids don't need to be deeply relating to their parents every moment or walking hand in hand through the zoo or playing educational games whenever they are together. Children need parents to *be there*. Kids learn how to live by watching the way their parents live. *Both* parents.

Here's where the "compromise" part comes in. Parents need to figure out ways to organize their lives so their children are *nurtured*, not just fed, housed, and clothed. Sit down with your spouse and a pad and pencil and get started. Calculate how much money you need to live, what you can do without, how much money each parent can bring in. Talk to your boss about flextime, working from home. Cut back to part-time, work nights after the kids have gone to bed, live with less luxury, make, bake, or borrow your needs. Once you accept the premise that raising kids is a two-parent deal—no fudging—you'll be amazed at the creative ways you *can* make it happen. Jane, I know it may be hard to relinquish the mommy reins. He's not going to be as good a "mom" as you are. He's not going to dress the kids the way you'd dress them or teach them everything you'd teach them. That's okay. He's *not* Mom, he's Dad. That's why having two parents who are involved in raising the kids is so important. Kids need balance, perspective, and most of all, hands-on parenting from the *two* people who brought them into the world. Understand that most men have been encouraged *not* to be hands-on dads; most women have been encouraged *not* to be providers. Give each other a break, be patient and supportive, and watch your children blossom under your example. It's not going to happen overnight, but *true* two-parent families are an ideal to work toward and something to be determined to achieve one way or another.

WILD THINGS

Q. *Parental sex roles are completely reversed when it comes to the:*
   a. Pink flamingo
   b. Sea horse
   c. Mongoose

A. *Sea horse.* One of the few examples of male "pregnancy," the female sea horse deposits thousands of eggs into a male sea horse's internal pouch, where he fertilizes the eggs and carries them to term. After a two-week gestation period, he expels the baby sea horses by contracting his pouch. In this case, nature has determined that the father is more capable of carrying, feeding, and protecting the young than the mother is. While human fathers are capable of raising their young as well, the healthiest families have a male *and* female parental role model . . . even if the roles are reversed.

Q. *When it comes to incubating their young, which animal has devised a perfect fifty-fifty split of parental responsibility?*
   a. Sea otter
   b. Ostrich
   c. Dolphin

A. *Ostrich.* These birds have taken their heads *out* of the sand to coparent their hatching offspring. A female ostrich sits on her eggs by day, the father takes over at night. It's more than a good way for each parent to get a rest. The bigger, stronger males can more easily protect the eggs at night when more predators lurk in the darkness. Now, if they could just figure out a way to spend some time *together*, enjoying their relationship with each other, ostriches would be the perfect model for human parents!

Boys to Men

A S I SAID, both nature *and* nurture conspire against boys growing into men who become dads and actually *raise* the kids. It starts at the very beginning of life. Biologically, the real differences between males and females happen at about

the seventh month of gestation. That's when the hormones, genetics, and anatomy are in place establishing the sex of your little
cherub. Sociological and psychological differences between males
and females begin being created the moment your baby is born.

Without even realizing it, parents, other family members,
friends, teachers, rabbis, priests *teach* boys how to be "boys" and
girls how to be "girls" by the way they talk, act, react, feel, assume
things about and encounter your child.

In a study done twenty years ago, a researcher dressed a baby
in pink bunting, blue bunting, and yellow bunting on three suc-
cessive days. The researcher then videotaped people's reactions in
a grocery store. It was the same baby each time. There was no char-
acteristic about the baby that could tip people off as to sex—just the
color of the wardrobe. When people saw the pink bunting and
decided the baby was a girl, their voices got higher, and they used
words like *cute, delicate,* and *beautiful* to describe "her." When the
same baby was wrapped in the blue bunting, people dropped their
voices and called "him" a "bruiser" and "tough guy." They were
much more physically aggressive with the "boy" baby, more cuddly
with the "girl." And when they dressed the infant in yellow
bunting, the reactions were somewhere in between.

The fact is that we begin socializing our children very early
on—essentially from the time they come home from the hospital,
certainly the first time you dress that kid and the first time you
take him or her out in public. External cultural influences are so
powerful that even when parents make a conscious effort to sort of
neutralize their child, society takes over and teaches its version of
sex roles.

When my daughter was two and a half, she asked me if we
could go out and play. I said I couldn't because I had to go to work
and play doctor. She said, "You mean *nurse,* Mommy." I said no, I

mean doctor. She then told me that her friend Jeremy said girls can't be doctors, girls have to be nurses. I said, "Honey, I'm a doctor. I have a Ph.D. And I'm not a girl, I'm a woman." Then I realized I'm not even arguing with my two-year-old, but somebody else's!

So unless you keep your child locked in a rubber, windowless room, outside influences are going to be very powerful. When raising little boys, parents are under intense pressure to keep them "boylike." Think about it: Girls can be "tomboys," which garners grudging respect; they can wear pants and get muddy. A boy who defies the stereotypes gets called "sissy," or worse, "mama's boy."

Catch a little boy wearing a dress or playing quietly with a Barbie doll and most parents freak out. Or, at the very least, they try to steer their little boy toward more "boylike" activities, such as playing sports or Rollerblading. Boys have bicycles, trucks, things that move. Girls have dolls, thing that are passive. *Inner* toys. Relationship-building toys. Look at a tea service. A tea service isn't going anyplace. Boys have train sets, airplanes—toys that encourage action and aggression. Anything short of being absolutely "male"—dominantly, aggressively, bullyish *male*—is unacceptable. You can be an unfeminine girl and still be female; you cannot be an unmasculine boy and still be male.

The first identity crisis for a little boy starts between eighteen months and two years of age. Before this age, a child does not differentiate between self and other. At about two, children begin their first lurch toward independence. It's why the "terrible twos" are so hard for a first-time mom; her compliant little cherub is beginning to pull away and oppose her. Subsequent children will also have tantrums, but the veteran mom is more prepared and less sandbagged.

In this country, children are still predominantly raised by women. When a little girl commences that lurch, she can be independent and still identify with the dominant figure—her mom. She can say no and still be like Mom—dress like Mom, sound like Mom, act like Mom. It's reinforcing. It eases some of the fear inherent in breaking away from the person who takes care of you, who is responsible for your day-to-day survival. A little boy at the same age has a much more complicated task. He has to separate from Mom much more radically.

Even though he still wants to feel close and be loved, he can't identify with her or want to be like her without risking being a "mama's boy." He wants to be separate, his own person, but has to sever the link. It's scary being a boy all by himself, being *not* like Mom. By now he's learned that boys don't cry, that he should take it like a man, get out there and be aggressive. Little girls are encouraged to be passive, obedient, clean homebodies, frightened of mice, loud noises, and icky boys, cutesy, high-pitch-voiced, and petite. Boys are expected to be aggressive, tough, dirty, fearless, deep-throated, and muscular. In fact, even when boys do horrible things, when they are overly aggressive bullies, their behavior is written off as "boys will be boys." When girls exhibit the same behavior, they are told, "No one will marry you if you act that way."

This tender age is the beginning of a boy's emotional isolation. A father contributes to his son's burgeoning identity by showing that he feels the dominant characteristics his boy displays come from him. Any clinging behavior, any softness, he takes personally. He freaks out. He tries to whip him into shape. Any perceived weakness, like wetting the bed, for example (which is much more common in boys than in girls), is viewed as a slight against his own manhood. Real men have real sons who act real manly and don't wet the bed. Wetting the bed is a loss of control, and real men don't lose control, particularly of their penises.

Carl, forty-three, wrote to me with this very problem. His son, now a preteen, continues to wet the bed occasionally. "I've tried everything," he stated. "I wake him up before I go to bed to make sure he doesn't have to urinate. I ask him in the morning if I need to wash his sheets. I won't let him drink any liquid after eight P.M. What else can I do?"

Leave him alone, Carl. That's what you can do. Carl has inadvertently been shaming his son for years. He may have had the same problem himself—it's often genetic, but dads are too humiliated to ever admit it to their sons. The best way to handle any bedwetting situation is to remove the shame, understand that little boys are not as neurologically mature as little girls, don't take it personally, and let him change and wash his own sheets so he is taking care of his own self.

When little boys hit nursery school and come in contact with other little boys on a day-to-day basis, the struggle for dominance really starts. Boys have penises; they can stand up and "mark" the urinal. When they have recess, they can wrestle with one another. At this age, too, the emotional isolation heats up. Since most preschool and elementary-school teachers are women, little girls continue to be able to associate with the authority figure; boys continue to distance themselves. They can't associate with the women who take care of them because any feelings of closeness compromise their independence.

Feeling close to Mom means he's tied to her apron strings, so if he feels close to Ms. Smith, his favorite teacher, it has to be construed as a crush, as *sexual*, so this intimacy doesn't compromise his sexual identity. Little boys are encouraged to define feelings of warmth and closeness as primarily sexual from an age well before puberty, while girls can idolize a male or female teacher until well into high school without attaching "sexual" feelings to

the adoration. Early on for boys there's a dichotomy between intimacy and sex, with closeness to the first woman—Mom—being
both seductive and claustrophobic, not to mention unmanly. A
boy's best friend is his mother?

Later, these feelings can affect dating and mating behavior.
Feeling close to women feels scary. Sex without intimacy works
very well because intimacy means your manhood is at stake. Look
at all the hostile terms some men have for making love: screwing,
nailing, shagging. It's no wonder some men have problems with
intimacy. It's been set up since they were two years old. And marriage is no cure. Men talk about wives as "the old ball and chain,"
an appendage, marriage as an *institution*.

The solution for raising loving, nurturing boys? Fathers
need to more involved. Period. If Dad is around every day when
his boy is young, his son can identify with a *present* male, not
struggle to connect with an absent one. If there's no father
around, make sure there's a father *figure* available on a regular
basis. Big brother. Relatives. Friends. A male baby-sitter you can
trust. It's crucial to have positive, constant, consistent male influences in any child's life (male or female).

HIStory

HISTORICALLY, HAVING babies was a means for genetic
survival. Period. It wasn't a way to fulfill yourself or
experience the joys of parenthood. That's a fairly recent
phenomenon. Humans had kids to preserve their DNA. The very
word *reproduction* means creating yourself again.

Oddly enough, some anthropologists theorize that reproduction is one of the drives that fueled early male philandering. If a male caveman impregnated another female in a neighboring cave while his wife was raising his first family, he guaranteed a continuous supply of offspring and boosted his chances of launching his DNA into history. Not to mention the fact that childbirth was a very risky business. Lots of women didn't survive it, and lots of kids didn't make it far beyond babyhood.

Prehistoric life expectancy was about twenty to thirty years of age. Even thousands of years later, in medieval Europe, three to five out of every ten babies didn't survive beyond infancy. After that, a medieval baby had about a fifty-fifty chance of making it to a medieval grown-up. Plus, in those days, parenting was a considerably different matter. Beating a child for "disciplinary" reasons was the key to the parenting style of the day, and because this was the normal course of punishment, if the child died during the beating, parents weren't held liable for it.

So, men historically had a biological imperative to have as many offspring as possible, which isn't the same as a biological imperative to be good *dads* or caring, nurturing child-rearers. That job always has been a mommy thing.

The notion of boys getting "soft" by hanging around women too much is as old as time. Soft for what? The hunt, the kill, the harvest, the grueling workday. Native American males often took part in self-torture rituals to "toughen up" and convince the spirits that they were worthy of a bountiful hunt. In the Cheyenne eight-day Sun Dance, a dancer would have two holes cut into the skin of his chest, a skewer pushed through the holes, and a pole attached to the skewer by a rope. He'd dance with the pole all night until his skin broke, hoping to garner good fortune, social status, and approval.

Historically, fathers have raised their boys to be successful hunters, brave warriors, plentiful farmers, hard workers. Historically, mothers have raised their girls to be good *wives*.

The history of fathers and their offspring is really a story of ego and economics. Males want their genes to live on and prosper. That's ego. The only way to make sure that the child is really theirs is to keep a tight rein on its mother. That's economic. The best way to control someone is to control the purse strings. Keep her barefoot and pregnant (how far can she run without shoes?). Money is about control; controlling a woman is the only way a man could be sure that his offspring really meant it when they called him "Daddy."

The agrarian society that characterizes much of human history is the perfect example of male ego and economics at work. From the Neolithic farmers in 4,000 B.C. to pioneers in the American West, working the land was man's work; his children were his workforce. The bigger the land, the greater his status, the more pressing the need for "field hands" to help him maintain and expand his territory. Boys were put to work in the fields as soon as they could pick corn; their sisters were assigned to the farm kitchen as soon as they could shuck it. The family farm, family business, following in Father's footsteps is how the power and status stays in the male's primary power structure: his pride.

Ironically, the more children there are in a family, the more burden is placed on (usually) the father to provide for those kids. 'Cause that's what most dads have been raised to do: provide. So, historically, kids were both a financial burden on the family and a financial resource. Historically, fathers have considered their children allies in their often herculean efforts to provide for their families. Kids worked in factories or sweatshops as Charles Dickens did at age twelve. In 1824, his dad was thrown in debtor's prison and Charles was put to work at Warren's Shoe Blacking Factory. Since most males are not raised to nurture their young, putting their children to work for the good of the pride comes with the territory. It feels natural. The patriarch worked when he was a kid, his dad worked, his granddad worked, and, by golly, his sons are going to get out there and get a job as soon as it's legally possible, too. Even today, kids around the world are working in the fields or in sweatshops to put food on the family table.

Finally, understanding the history of men and their families is understanding the history of contraception. Being pregnant, having babies, raising babies, getting pregnant again kept women at home, out of men's hair, and away from the hubs of power. Attempts at birth control have been around since ancient Greece. Women used sea sponges, made linen condoms, even dried fish powder as a means to curtail unwanted pregnancy. One of the more unsavory early attempts at contraception was mixing dried, ground-up cow dung with honey as a sort of, ahem, natural spermicide. Few methods worked very well, and I do *not* recommend that you try these at home. . . .

Birth control stopped men's biological control in the bedroom and allowed women to both enjoy sex and escape the enslavement of biological destiny. Without viable, acceptable means of preventing pregnancy, men and women were both trapped in a vicious cycle of having kids, having more mouths to feed, and enlisting the kids' help in feeding, housing, and clothing the family. The pressure was on Dad to bring home the bacon, on Mom to fry it up in a pan and be sexually available to her man should he desire a little nooky for dessert.

The point is, women have been trying to practice family

planning since they realized how expensive, time-consuming, tiring, and disenfranchising raising children can be. Nothing breeds dissatisfaction faster than when both men and women view women as financially dependent baby-makers. I'm convinced that once women view themselves as viable economically, they'll stop having babies to define themselves. If you give women a way to feel important other than by having babies, they will. Which means that Jane's husband no longer has to bear the total bone-chilling financial responsibility alone—he has a helpmate and partner in the fullest sense of the word. This allows him to live not only longer, but happier as well. He even gets treated to a night on the town every once in a while.

Men and Their Families

THE NOTION THAT women want families more than men simply isn't true. The drive to procreate is as strong in men as it is in women. The difference is that most males haven't been taught how to *raise* the kids they've made. Men are taught to roar in the jungle, not purr at home. They've been trained to kill the enemy, not cuddle with the cubs. Feelings are the enemy. They are "excuses" for failure.

Guys have internalized the idea that a man is a *provider.* He provides sustenance, not emotions. That soft stuff comes from Mom. But watch out, the thinking goes—too much time around women will soften *you.* It'll make you vulnerable to more aggressive males. You'll lose your status, be shunned from the pack.

Since fathers rarely talk with one another about their parenting skills, hardly ever take parenting classes, seldom sweat and fret as much about being a good dad as moms do, they are more lockstepped when it comes to parenting. Men raise kids the way they were raised, the way their fathers were raised, the way their grandfathers and their great-grandfathers were raised. There simply isn't the opportunity to rethink what they're doing and make the changes that will improve not only their kids' lives, but their children's kids' lives as well.

A thirty-seven-year-old guy called my program with a problem. "My wife wants me to have dinner with the kids every night," he said. I asked him how old his kids were and he said, "Six, eight, and ten." Then I asked the obvious question: "Why would you *not* want to eat with your kids?" He confessed that his father had never eaten dinner with him. When I asked if he'd wanted to eat dinner with his dad, he started to cry. He was flabbergasted. He didn't know where the tears came from. I said, "Listen, you have to do three things. Number one, to save your marriage, you're going to have to accommodate your wife. Suggest having dinner with the kids two or three times in the next week. Otherwise, you're not going to have much of a marriage. Number two, you need to do some business with your dad. Find out what his behavior was all about. You felt divorced from your father; find out why. Number three, spend more time with your kids. Find time to be with each child individually. Your children need you."

He said he'd give it a try. A few weeks later, he called me back. "You changed my life," he said. "You saved my marriage. I feel like I've put down years of burden."

His burden, and the burden of anyone who isn't encouraged to explore his or her emotional life, is the weight of history, genetics, and learned behavior. Evolution is slow, particularly when your behavior sort of works for you. In most cases in our culture, what works best for a man—what gains him the most status, the best sex—is being a lion at work, not a pussycat at home. Until everybody joins the party, until women and bosses and other guys and movie heroes and busty young bimbettes think it's sexy and cool for a man to share kid duty fifty-fifty, men are going to go for the *gold,* not the diaper pail.

Working It Out Together

RAISING CHILDREN can't be "women's work" anymore. It simply doesn't cut it with all we now know about family dynamics. On the other hand, women can't expect men to drop out of the workforce for eighteen years to become at-home dads. Historically, the Mr. Mom phenomenon hasn't worked very well for either sex. Females often feel disenfranchised, financially insecure, an appendage to their husbands when they are "trapped" at home with the kids. Why put the same burden on men? Plus, the family model of Mom in the kitchen and Dad in the boardroom isn't any more appropriate than one of Dad in the kitchen and Mom in the boardroom. Raising kids must be a *shared* responsibility if we want our children to have the best possible shot at a full, happy, loving, giving life. For most families, this means rethinking the whole setup.

Jane, being a good mother means making sure your kids spend a lot of time with their dad as well as their mom. If he works all the time, it's time for you to get a job and help him out. Make a deal with him: For every hour you work to supplement your income, he spends a half hour hanging out with the kids. And assigning only grunt work, like driving Susie to ballet or picking up more diapers on the way home from work, isn't fair to your husband or your kids. They both deserve fun time with one another.

Tarzan, I know it can feel scary to think about reducing the number of hours you work so you can spend more time with the kids. Or if you don't work, or are out of work and looking for a job, I know money worries seem all-consuming. But you have the right to expect your wife to share the financial load just as you share the child-rearing duties. Neither one of you has to feel as though you're in it alone. Once you accept the fact that kids need their dads as much as they need their moms, you'll find a way to make it work.

If you're a *single* mom, Jane, you certainly know that raising kids alone can be lonely, exhausting, expensive, and not much fun sometimes. On the other hand, it's often satisfying to see what you can do on your own. While you may have been trained from birth to be Donna Reed (remember those Easy Bake ovens?) or Murphy Brown (no matter what Dan Quayle says), understand that kids need men *and* women in their lives in order to grow up emotionally, psychologically, and socially solid. Make sure your kids are around great guys, who aren't necessarily dates, on a regular basis. Heaven knows it's hard enough to get a great guy to *date* or hang around Mom, much less hang around the kids, but it's important to make it a priority. Kids need both male and female role models. Men are *not* sperm donors; they contribute substantially to the psyches of our kids. It's every parent's job to make sure to create the best possible environment in which those psyches can flourish.

Making hard choices is what parenting is all about. Kids are sponges, incredibly susceptible to parental influence. While it often seems as though they're not listening (and they probably aren't most of the time), your kids are always watching, learning, interpreting, and deciphering cues from both parents. You can't *say* you want your children not to smoke, for example, if you smoke yourself. You can't expect them to treat their siblings with respect if you yell at your spouse. Parenting is all about setting a living, breathing example of the way you want your kids to turn out. I know it's not easy—it's difficult most of the time—but parents have a deep responsibility to their children, themselves, and the *world* to take parenting seriously enough to do it well.

QUANTUM

MEN	WOMEN
Remember your fondest memory of your dad.	Let your kids be in charge for one whole day.
Remember your biggest high-school disappointment.	Take a day to indulge yourself.
How did you disappoint your dad?	For one week, pay ten dollars anytime you criticize any household member.
Bake something with your kids.	Let him dress the kids for his events.
Allow your wife to blindfold you when you're both dressed.	Do something as a couple that would ordinarily be "family"—like camping, going out for dinner, taking a trip to the beach, going to church or synagogue.
	Don't mediate between him and the kids.

LEAPS

Four

The Pack

Men and Friendship

W HEN CHIMPANZEES are playing, they start by opening their eyes wide, covering their teeth with their lips, and stretching their mouths open in a goofy grin. Then they hang upside down and show their friends a silly "play face" that soundlessly communicates to them that, "Hey, guys, when I slap you or tackle you or nibble on your hairy arm, I'm just kidding, okay?" When they see this, their buddies know the score. They don't confuse play—no matter how rough it gets—with war, though their monkeying around can get a mite physical sometimes.

That's okay. Chimps will be chimps. Their roughhousing is not only fun and games, it's a training ground for real battles later on.

When human male friends gather at the sports stadium, their eyes open wide and their lips stretch in a goofy grin. They paint their faces in the color of their favorite football team, wear their team's cheese hat or jersey, or play at chopping their opponent's neck. They slap their friends' backs and pummel one another with each score. At home watching a football game, they scream at the television set, growl at the referee, holler at the players. (A very different kind of hollering is aimed at any *woman* or *child* foolish enough to interrupt their game.)

For three hours, it's *war.* The quarterback fires a *bullet,* the defensive line tries to *sack* him, the offensive line struggles to advance into enemy territory. But the guys are cool; they know all the violence is only play. When it's all over, the living room or the Super Dome looks like a battlefield of broken tortilla chips and smashed pizza boxes. The victors celebrate, the losers commiserate. And the maidens clean it all up.

Understanding men and their friends—their pack—means exploring the very definition of male intimacy. With men, intimacy is a *physical* experience. Guys feel close when they are shoulder to shoulder, side by side, in the same room, car, bed, playground, field, bleachers; women feel close when they are connecting emotionally. For women, talking with their friends, thinking about them, writing to them—but especially *talking*—really works. With men, intimacy is about *doing* something together, not just *feeling* close. It's why women can maintain friendships over the phone and men need to hang with their homeboys. Physical proximity is what it's all about. It's how men feel connected and respected and cared for without feeling threatened. Well, without feeling *too* threatened.

Look, being male means being on guard, always feeling threatened. Males have been schooled to be competitive—somebody's *always* on your tail. It's the nature of men to continuously feel the need to prove themselves to one another, their dads, their moms, their wives, girlfriends, teachers, lovers, teammates, bosses, the guys at the gym, the girls on the bus.

Men have a running tally in their heads of who's up, who's down. It's why they memorize sports statistics and can spout reams of seemingly (at least to women) useless trivia. It's why guys argue with one another about *anything.*

One of my male friends admitted to me that his relationship with his best friend is built on *bets*—"I bet I can guess how far away that building is" or "I bet I can bench-press more than you" or "I bet she won't call you back." He confessed that a good part of the fun is reminding the "loser" how many times he's beat him.

A man's competitive nature is the reason he'll do almost anything to avoid looking foolish, for looking foolish means you're losing points.

In an ironic twist, guys who are nibbling at the edge of the "treating women as equals" cookie may carry that point-counting thing into their male/female goings-on. For example, a man may informally keep score of who's won the "I can stand to see my socks on the floor longer than you can" contest or the *"You* get up and fix the coffee, *dammit"* war. Yo, Jane, remember, taking turns takes the tension out of scorekeeping. And a giggle never hurts, either.

Competition among males is an animal thing, it's a human thing, it's probably an extraterrestrial thing, too. It just *is.* But men competing with their male friends can also be a *confusing* thing, especially if they're good at it. Not only does it feel lousy to lose, but while winning feels immediately terrific, it can be really lonely at the top. Once you get there, you've got to *stay* there. (There's only *one* Alpha male and a whole lotta wanna-bes.) So the competition continues on and on and a guy can never really let his guard down because, hey, his friends are competitive, too, and his best buddy may really be an Alpha wolf in sheep's (or Beta's) clothing. A human male is still human and he needs social contact like any other living organism. But man, oh man, it's scary.

Feeling close is expensive, dangerous comfort. *Yikes.* So what's a man to do? The male answer: Be close to another guy in terms of *physical* proximity, but keep your distance emotionally—don't talk about vulnerable, frightening things like *feelings.* Hang in groups (there's safety in numbers), play team sports (it's the only time you can be manly and still say hi to your mom, kiss the guys, cry, and pat one another on the butt), and make sure they see you sweat. Leave all the chatter to the girls.

For men, silence is not only golden, it's *survival.* Talking is giving out information, and giving out information is dangerous. Information identifies your position, it's aid to the enemy, and the enemy—or at least the competition—is everywhere. Men feel constantly at risk of attack. At any moment, a younger, stronger male could take his job, his woman, his manhood. Talking to someone requires eye contact; the focus is *forward.* You can't watch your back; you can't keep your eye on the competition. Guys feel the need to be on alert at all times, ever vigilant, ever wary. Even at play. *Especially* at play, when everything seems so friendly.

Jane, getting your big, strong lug involved in a noncompetitive "game" that doesn't allow for winning or losing—maybe squirting each other with a garden hose—gives him a chance to truly play without worrying about looking foolish. (Okay, I admit, I had a difficult time coming up with even *one* example of "play" that a man couldn't turn into a competition!)

Ever wonder why . . .

. . . guys choose the seat in a restaurant with the back against the wall? Because it *feels* safe. It's one reason men still pull chairs out for women—it allows them to control where she sits and where *he* sits.

Animal Instincts

FROM A ZOOLOGIST'S point of view, animals play with one another for two obvious reasons: to learn survival skills and to giggle—or at least the animal equivalent. Your dog romping in the park with a stick in his mouth is the picture of unbridled, spontaneous, infectious, delicious, pure joy (you should pardon the expression). Grab one end of the stick and Fido will growl, dig his haunches in the dirt, lower his front paws, twist his head back and forth, and pull. It's still a game, great fun and all that, but the moment competition enters the picture, we get growling, ruffled fur, serious intensity, focus—it becomes *war* play. In fact, the game is called tug-of-*war*. (I've played tug-of-war with my basset hound, beagle, Irish setter, and various mutts I've loved, and I swear all of them would rather lose their teeth than let go of the stick.) When my pooch would finally wrestle the stick away from me (I'm a girl; I let 'em win), he would often as not nail it to the ground with his paw and ferociously strip the bark off with his teeth. He had his "kill" and was ripping the "skin" off.

Games of controlled violence are an integral part of animal behavior, particularly with the young. Young lions swat at one another and playfully neck-bite; bears stand on their hind legs and wrestle; a male ibex rears up on his back hooves, enticing his buddies to join him in a mock fight by banging their bodies together. These "fights" rarely end in injury but teach young animals the limits of their strength, how to anticipate the enemy's moves, how to defend themselves. It's practice for, and crucial to, survival. In the *human* animal kingdom, junior war games are played out in Little League, schoolyard basketball, or Pop Warner Football.

What could be a better metaphor for war than football? Two sides line up and battle each other for territory. The injured are carried off the field; the victors are heroes, and they always get the girl.

A few years ago, I played on a basketball team with a bunch of middle-aged guys. The league rule was that you had to have at least one female per team. I'd put on my shorts and show up ready for a little fun, a little exercise—send me in, Coach, I'm ready to play—but it wasn't *play* for the guys, it was *war.* It was the most basic form of "whose is bigger." I mean, c'mon, what would Freud say about a game where guys have to *dunk* the ball through the cylindrical hoop? On the court, status, manhood, competition—the whole range of manliness was being played out before my eyes. The blue-collar guys thought they were more manly than the white-collar "wimps." The white-collar guys felt a sense of superiority because they made more money. From the first day, I was the only one playing for fun; every one of these guys was playing for blood.

I became really good at shooting from midcourt because it was a lot less dangerous and smelly than under the net. Besides, you got three points and everybody looked surprised and cheered wildly!

Sports is where men can release their animal natures. Sit courtside at a professional basketball game and it even *sounds* like the jungle—growling, grunting, spitting, hissing. Sports is an arena where men are free to do what men like to do best: prove who's King of the Jungle.

Animals that are *prey* instead of *predator* play war games as well. The difference is that their games are rehearsals for escape. Young red deer join one another in fake chases and display phony warning signals that danger is approaching. It's the human equivalent of playing cowboys and Indians, with some animals being the "good guys" and some animals being the "bad guys" and both sides learning how to survive.

Pack animals play *pecking order* games as a way to teach one another how to recognize and respect the Alpha males. Young animals play with older animals to learn just how far they can go without being reprimanded with a stinging swat upside the head. They also learn how to spot weakness and take full advantage. (Ever see a lion cub pounce on a sleeping elder? If they're big enough and fast enough, they get away with it.)

Animals play to prove who's hot and who's not. Play is a way for them to assert dominance—that top-dog *thang*. Animal play is the equivalent of boys hotdogging, getting picked for the team, earning a varsity letter, becoming a team player, standing out from the crowd, or being embarrassed for striking out. It's how young skinny males develop into strong manly studs, it's how boys learn to get along with one another. It's how the full human spectrum is developed and nurtured.

In the late sixties, a physician named Stuart Brown in the Department of Psychiatry at Baylor College of Medicine in Houston, Texas, was asked to figure out why a twenty-five-year-old student named Charles Joseph Whitman took an arsenal of guns to the top floor of the university's twenty-seven-story tower and started firing. He killed thirteen people and wounded thirty-one before he was finally arrested. After interviewing the gunman's friends and family, Dr. Brown discovered that Charlie—an altar boy, an Eagle Scout, a Marine—had never really been allowed to *play*. His domineering, abusive father had controlled him so completely, he'd had no time to play.

JUNGLE GEMS

Understanding men and their friends means accepting these basic male notions:

+ *Men are competitive creatures.*
+ *Competitive creatures crave intimacy just as everyone else does.*
+ *Creating intimacy by sharing feelings feels unmanly.*
+ *Sharing feelings is giving a powerful weapon to someone; vulnerability is a statement of weakness.*
+ *Giving someone power increases vulnerability.*
+ *Weakness means an attack could be demolishing.*
+ *Men have learned that it's safer and smarter to create intimacy with* physical *proximity, not verbal exchange.*
+ *Physical proximity also allows men to keep an eye on one another—a friend could become a foe.*
+ *Men feel close to their friends by* hanging out *with them.*

After that revelation, Dr. Brown did a study of twenty-six convicted murderers in Texas and found that 90 percent of them had either no playtime as kids, or had exhibited abnormal play behavior such as sadism, torturing animals, being a bully, or teasing others relentlessly. He discovered that play is both an important component of a happy, healthy childhood as well as a valuable indicator of future sociability or, chillingly, pathology. He also discovered that playful adults were among the most creative, brilliant people. It's no accident that our animal instincts to play are so strongly embedded in our human DNA.

Boys to Men

WHEN THAT LURCH toward independence begins around age two, human animals begin the big breakaway from their parents. Since Mommy is most often the primary caretaker, that means kids are breaking free of Mom. It's a scary time, made even more scary for little boys, who have to create a totally separate identity that doesn't look, sound, smell, or, heaven forbid, dress like Mom. Little boys who *don't* break away from their moms are called "sissies" and "mama's boys" and are beaten up by the tough, manly boys on the block. So early on little boys learn what's "girlish" and what's not. Moms talk; dads clam up. Feelings are feminine. Moms cry when they watch a sad movie, dads maintain a stiff upper lip. Moms are kissy-face and huggy and touchy and feely; at best, dads tousle hair, pat backs, and hug briefly.

The tension at this early age is all about the struggle between intimacy and independence. Boys long to feel close to their mothers, the women who care for and nurture them and make them feel safe and special, but there's some behavior that's acceptable and some that isn't. Hugging Mom is still okay; crying and telling her you miss her and love her and want to be just like her isn't. Being physical is okay; being verbal, especially if it's to whine or complain, is too sissy to be okay. And independence is about walking away altogether.

So the struggle really becomes one of *physical* proximity versus isolation. Since crying for attention, whining, or chattering isn't okay for male children, boys can feel intimate just being in the same room with Mom without saying those words that would brand them as unmanly. They often seem involved in their own play, but can suddenly disengage if Mom leaves and therefore follow her to another room (because being alone is so scary). Little girls don't have to pull away from Mom in the same way that boys do. They can be independent yet still be exactly like the woman they love.

Look at the difference between girls' and boys' birthday parties from grade school on. Little girls' birthday parties involve lots of friends, and they often organize surprise parties. They wear fancy patent-leather shoes and party dresses, and they sit around and giggle and squeal with delight as they open each new gift. Little boys tend to do something active, like go bowling, with their best friend or just a few friends. They build a shared experience physically, instead of sitting around and talking about the experience as it happens. Girls say, "Isn't this fun!" Boys don't say anything, but indicate to one another the fact that they're having a good time by boisterously affirming their presence with one another—running around, hitting one another, hollering. If a guy isn't having fun, he leaves. If a girl isn't having fun, she whines.

Ever wonder why . . .

. . . guys hate surprise parties? When women say, "Don't do anything for my birthday," they really mean "Do something lavish, just don't tell anyone my age." When guys say, "Don't do anything for my birthday," they mean it. *Don't do anything for my birthday.* Guys dislike surprise parties because they don't like being out of control. A surprise means you don't know what's going to happen next. It means you're vulnerable, you have to go with the flow. Most men prefer knowing the rules in advance so they can feel prepared.

Early on, boys are taught that physical contact is as close to intimacy as they are going to get. They learn to "hug" by socking one another in the arm, and tell friends how they feel about them by calling them "jerk" or "doofus" or "wimp." Think of E-mail and phone sex as the adult manifestations of these young behaviors: It's on a computer or phone ("manly," complicated electronics), at arm's length (safe), anonymous (nonthreatening—it's not *really* me), with someone with whom I don't have to make eye contact (I don't have to feel vulnerable), connected yet completely separate, protected, and in control (I can hang up or sign off anytime I feel the need). They offer a false, but safe, sense of intimacy.

Boys also learn about pack behavior as kids. They join *teams;* team leaders establish a pecking order by choosing the fittest teammates first, then whittling down to the weakest link. The ultimate insult? Not being picked for a team. Which means you haven't measured up, you're being shunned by the pack. You're *bottom* dog and everybody knows it.

The team, or pack, mentality teaches boys to establish their place (their position), follow the rules, and trust that others will watch your back. It's not that little girls don't also have a rigid social structure, but it's based much less on performance—the ability to tell a joke or hit a ball or run fast. The performance criterion means the team, or pack, has a place and a value (although the value can vary greatly), so teammates learn to feel safe surrounded by the gang. Players who veer outside the team format are labeled "hotdoggers"—they think they're so hot they can survive without the pack. Interestingly, even when hotdoggers score one for the team, their coach and teammates chastise them. The message is that winning isn't as important as maintaining the team structure. Unity is where safety lies. It's how young pack members grow up to maintain and respect the pack structure in everyday life.

Think about it: Employees are praised for being "team players," for *not* being a lone wolf or vulture. While achieving top-dog status is rewarded—even if the rules are broken—the price for falling short of top-dog status is severe. Better to know your place, be one of the guys. The group will turn on, brutalize, and shun a public "failure." There is no sympathy and no quarter given, perhaps because the failed male represents the ultimate male fear—there but for the grace of God go I!

That's what gangs are all about—joining a *team*, having others to watch your back. Just like with any other team, with gangs there are secret signs and signals, uniforms, ways to identify friend and foe. There is scoring, evening the score, turf battles. Gangs have their dugouts, their haunts, their equivalent of the sports bar or locker room. Often for boys without a father figure, becoming part of a gang is an attempt to have some semblance of male intimacy in their lives. It's a way for them to feel close to a male role model. Gangs are a way for boys to *be* men. They will literally die for one another because they feel dead *without* one another.

The upswing in violence in the last few decades is not coincidental to the increase of fatherless families. Boys with no Alpha male at home to emulate and try to topple can become supermacho predators looking for "prey" in the outside world. The only parental intimacy possible is with Mom, which makes you a "mama's boy," so the feeling is "I have to prove to the world that I'm *really* not." At the same time, though, it's important to hang on to the one source of intimacy possible, so saying "your mama" is fighting words. Calling a guy an SOB is an affectionate insult; impugning his mama by calling him a "bastard" is not. The idea that your father abandoned you, denied you, hits the very core of manhood itself.

WILD THINGS

Q. *When elephants of different sizes play together, the larger elephant:*

    a. Immediately assumes the dominant position.

    b. Adjusts his height to "fit" the smaller elephant.

    c. Declines to play with his "inferior."

A. *Adjusts his height to "fit" the smaller elephant.* Elephants, like humans, believe in a fair fight—even if it's only playful warfare. Larger elephants often kneel to accommodate smaller elephants with whom they spar. It's as if winning doesn't really count unless the playing field is level. Human male animals feel the same way. Competing isn't really competitive unless guys have a worthy adversary. That's why (with the notable exception of sumo wrestling) weight classes are established, there are minor and major leagues, regular and postseason play, all-star games, handicapping, seeded players, and slow and fast lanes on the freeway.

Q. *In most animals, the difference between the "play face" and the aggressive, angry face is the:*
    a. Eyes.
    b. Lips.
    c. Teeth.

A. *Teeth.* Happy, playful animals bare more lip than fang. In fact, most animals actually "smile" when they're happy by stretching their lips over their teeth. Angry animals, like angry humans, signal their displeasure by opening their mouths widely and exposing their sharp teeth. It's the animal version of hollering—chewing somebody out, biting his head off. As in humans, animal body language signifies friend or foe. Just as a human would only reluctantly approach a grimacing man, an animal would be wary of messing with any animal flashing his pearly whites.

Q. *Social animals, like the horse or mountain goat, rarely play by themselves.*
    a. True
    b. False

A. *False.* Animals often play by themselves, literally leaping for joy. That's where the terms "horsing around," "kidding around," and "monkeying around" come from. One animal researcher even spotted a raven sliding down a snowy hillside in Wales, flat on his back. He thought it was an accident until he watched the raven climb back up to the top and slide down again. Hippos have been spotted doing underwater back flips, and desert mice often jump for joy in the moonlight. Most animals, like humans, need all sorts of playtime in order to thrive and lead happy, productive lives.

HIStory

THE HISTORY OF men hanging out with their friends is the history of either work, war, public drinking, or athletics. Athletics is, and was, a metaphor and substitute for *war*. A month before the early Olympic Games, an international truce was declared among all Greeks so that competing athletes could get to Olympia safely. According to one Greek myth, the Olympic Games themselves were conceived by Zeus to celebrate the fact that he had wrestled control of the world away from his dad, Cronus. Sports was a way for men and gods to pound their chests and say, "I'm king of the world!" Or, more important, to say, "I'm better than you." From those clever ancient Greeks who figured out that the best way to exclude women from their competitive games was to compete in the nude (supposedly the fairer sex couldn't handle seeing all that brawn and sweat), to early Virginian settlers who inflated a sheep's bladder just to kick it around the fields, sports has been a testosterone thing, a way for guys to hang out with guys, to feel close, elevate their status, be needed, prove their manhood, keep aggression within acceptable limits.

Organized sports has always been linked to men socializing with one another. The Greek wrestling school of Plato's day, the *palaestra*, was one of the hottest hangouts around. After musing about politics and those pesky Spartans, men would work out, then clean themselves by rubbing oil all over their naked bodies and scraping the mix of oil, dirt, and sweat off their bodies with a special long, thin tool called a strigil. No women were allowed. No wonder! (No snickering about strigils, please!)

Other early sports, like the pre-baseball game of rounders, and bare-knuckled boxing, sometimes were a fight to the finish. In rounders, outfielders were allowed to put (and knock!) runners out by beaning them with a hard ball as they ran around the bases. Early boxers were allowed to wear a thin, metal-studded glove over their knuckles to maim and occasionally kill their opponents. Of course, modern boxing isn't all that different if you consider the fact that a knockout means a guy's brain has been literally knocked into the back of his cranial cavity and rendered him unconscious (and incredibly vulnerable, to say the least!).

It's easy to see why so many men resist the notion of women competing against them. When left to their own devices, the male competitive nature can get pretty intense. When guys want women to understand that they *like* it that way, that they feel close when they're beating each other's brains in (or watching some other guys do it), and that women should just be quiet and refill the Doritos bowl, you can see where a conflict can arise. Women view sports violence as a by-product; men often view it as the *point.* If you don't believe me, look at how the fans behave at soccer games, hockey games, or during the aftermath of championship celebrations.

Men and Their Friends

MALE FRIENDSHIPS and female friendships are obviously vastly different. *Duh.* No revelations here. Males seek physical proximity to feel close, while females rely on verbal communication—you can see where friendships between men and women can get tricky. When it comes to adult males and their adult (ahem) friendships, the differences can be even more striking.

Marjorie, thirty-four, called my program to ask me why on earth guys like *golf*. "I just don't get it," she said. "My husband disappears for hours, says he's exercising, says he's networking, but all he's really doing is standing around in silence waiting for his turn to hit a little ball into a little hole. What could be more boring?"

Marjorie's call illustrates the difference between men and women. Without even realizing it, she had just stated exactly *why* men like golf. They get to disappear for hours, stand around in silence, shoulder to shoulder, with their buddies. When they do talk, it's in quick spurts about work, politics, the last shot. They don't need to figure out something to say, as they might be required to do with a woman who needs some sign or proof of intimacy. Their intimacy is all right there, in the sunshine, on the green, in the quiet of the game. Plus, they can prove their manhood by driving their ball into the same hole. What could be better? I can remember going off for a romantic weekend with a relatively new beau. I was trying to establish our "*us*ness" by commenting on his car, the scenery, music we liked in common. He turned to me and said, "We don't have to talk." Well, I guess it depends on your DNA. My feelings were hurt, while he just wanted to not have to think.

Male and female friendships differ in another crucial area: bird-dogging. Bird-dogging is when a guy goes after his best friend's girl, something most women find abhorrent. But with men, it's a mixed bag. A man definitely wants his friends to approve of and admire his woman. How many guys are going to go after a woman their buddies have labeled a "dog" or "slut"? So when a guy has a good woman, he's elevated his status in the pack. To the other males—forever his competitors—his woman already has the Good Housekeeping Seal of Approval, so naturally she's even more attractive. And stealing someone's mate increases your status. If you can lure a woman away from your best friend, you're more of an Alpha male than he is.

Several years ago, I took a survey of men and women, asking, "If you knew your spouse was having an affair with your best friend, who would you be madder at?" Women blamed the woman, and men blamed the woman. Why? Because women place an entirely different value on friendship—stealing a man is the ulti-mate breach—and most men have a sacred bond with one another that few women can disrupt. You tend to blame the least valu-able person, and both men and women value men over women. This is sometimes rationalized by saying, "Well, you know *men*— they think with their *little* head. It's up to the woman to set the rules." *Yech.*

Look at the male and female side of a wedding party. A man has a "best man" to "stand up" for him. He's the *best* male in the kingdom. A woman has bridesmaids—minions to take care of her, to smooth out her train. And she has a maid of honor. *Honor* for females is synonymous with *chastity.* Guys have the best possible male in the pack; women have the maid.

Working It Out Together

WHEN IT COMES to couples dealing with men and their friends, women complain that men spend too much time with their friends (and away from her), while men complain that women smother them and try to keep them on a leash. The bottom-line issue for both sides is really about *time*. If there were forty-eight hours in a day, women wouldn't care if men spent a few hours with their friends; guys wouldn't feel guilty about hanging with their homeys if they had plenty of time left over to help out at home or tickle their mate's toes beneath the table in a candlelit restaurant on Saturday night. So, number one, couples need to make sure they have their *proportions* right. If every spare minute is set aside for *male* bonding, guys can bet there won't be much happiness (or female *bedding*) at home.

Looking at the amount of time guys spend with their friends is important. A ball game here and there, drinks after work now and then, a golf game on a Saturday afternoon is okay; *every day* is not. A man who needs or wants to spend every day—or almost every day—hanging out with the guys may have a deeper problem in his relationship with his woman. If a man is avoiding coming, or staying, home, it's important to figure out why.

Number two, understanding that *playtime* is an integral part of a happy lifetime—for both men and women—is crucial. Play builds intimacy, it relieves stress, it makes life worth living. Remember, all work and no play makes Jack a dull boy. Who wants a dull, unhappy man on her hands? Not only allowing men playtime, without taking it personally, but finding some for yourself is critical for women. Most men aren't "leaving her" to be with them;

he's just being with them. A woman standing between her man and his friends is a losing proposition. And a woman who says, "It's them or me," is making a mistake. Men almost always lash out when slapped with an ultimatum. Besides, a monogamous relationship means forsaking all others *sexually*, it doesn't mean solitary confinement.

Jane, if you think your man spends too much time with his friends, chill out. Spend some time with *your* friends, get a facial, eat crackers in bed. Whining about it, nagging, complaining, putting your foot down will only drive him out the door faster. He may feel smothered (or worse, *mothered*) around you, he may feel like the handyman or the sloppy child who messes everything up just as you clean everything up, or he may just like being with men who innately understand his need for silence, his need to compete, to scratch, pick his nose, untuck his shirt, uncover his bald spot, and let loose.

The best way to keep your man at home, or by your side, is to create a place where he *wants* to be. Hint: Guys rarely want to be at the fabric store picking out curtains (unless it's next to Home Depot). Figure out activities you both enjoy (he builds a tree house for the kids; you do the interior design) or set aside stuff you can do quietly next to him while he reads the paper or channel-surfs. Needlepoint, anyone? Or finish up the work you never get a chance to finish up at work. Understand that just *being there*, by his side, makes him feel close to you. Resist the urge to *tell* him how close you feel, too, and he'll soon long for quiet evenings at home with you.

Tarzan, if your Jane wants you to hang out with her more often, try scheduling time with her the same way you'd schedule a business meeting. Ask her out on a date, pencil her into your calendar, pencil yourself into hers. Understand that women often feel as if they're being pulled in all directions at once. The direction she'd most like to go, however, is right into your arms. Don't worry that she'll start demanding every extra minute of your day. A little goes a long way. Women want what you want: to feel loved, cherished, cared for. She's just more verbal about it than you are. The next time you want to hang out with the guys, you might want to try telling her how much you adore her, but you need to sit in the woods and bang drums and sweat with your men friends sometimes, too. Leaving her with the image of grubby, sweaty men alone in a forest together is much better than the one she probably has of drooling, sweaty guys together in a bar. Once you reassure her that you're not *escaping*, not sneaking out to ogle other women, not planning to join a fraternity and chug brewskies with the boys, she'll understand that you need time to bond with your buddies just as she does.

Jane, women who'd rather be with their man than with anyone else have a hard time understanding why their man doesn't feel the same. But, of course, the answer is, he's *not* the same—not exactly a news flash. If women don't allow men to be men, they end up with unhappy little boys, and unhappy little boys often act out and act up and exact revenge and treat wives like mothers. Women have to trust their men or leave 'em. If the only way a man can be trusted is within eyesight, everybody's going to feel claustrophobic. A dose of male bonding can't be looked upon as female rejection. The fear that guys in a group will do stuff that guys on their own would never do is not completely paranoid (just look at gangs or any kind of mob behavior), but women still have to trust their men enough to unlock the front door. A man who can't wait to escape the house so he can join his buddies at a bar or a strip club is a man who's not ready for a mature relationship with a woman— no matter how hard she tries to coerce him into it. It's not going to work. Her time is better spent finding a man who likes golf or *Monday Night Football* and, most important, spending time (not 24/7, but *time*) with her.

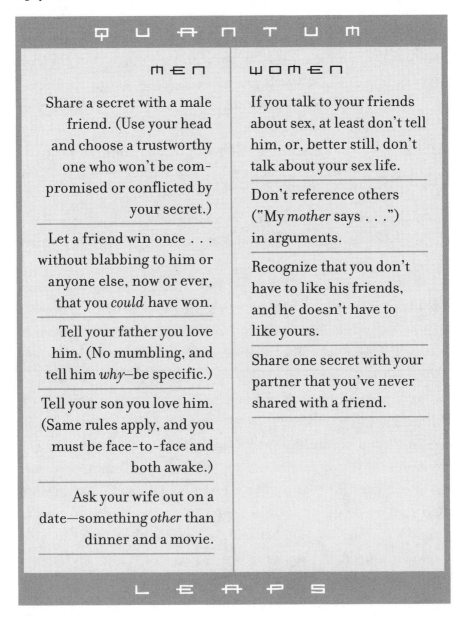

QUANTUM

MEN	WOMEN
Share a secret with a male friend. (Use your head and choose a trustworthy one who won't be compromised or conflicted by your secret.)	If you talk to your friends about sex, at least don't tell him, or, better still, don't talk about your sex life.
Let a friend win once . . . without blabbing to him or anyone else, now or ever, that you *could* have won.	Don't reference others ("My *mother* says . . .") in arguments.
Tell your father you love him. (No mumbling, and tell him *why*—be specific.)	Recognize that you don't have to like his friends, and he doesn't have to like yours.
Tell your son you love him. (Same rules apply, and you must be face-to-face and both awake.)	Share one secret with your partner that you've never shared with a friend.
Ask your wife out on a date—something *other* than dinner and a movie.	

LEAPS

Five

Locking Horns
Men and Conflict

C OMBATIVE MALE African gazelles perform a sort of "war" dance. They first circle each other warily, each hoping that when the other sees the length of his manly horns, he'll back down. If neither one does, they both flash their white barrel chests and turn their heads sideways, giving their opponent one more look at the size of their horns (yes, size matters in *every* species). If that still isn't enough to avert a fight, they go at it— charging, butting heads, locking horns.

Like males everywhere, male gazelles fight over the usual: territory or *girl* gazelles. Which turns out to be the same thing. Studly gazelles with a gazillion girls are the most powerful, most respected, most feared and revered gazelles on the savannah.

Two guys clashing in a pool hall perform a sort of war dance, too. They circle the table warily, calculating whether they can take the other one down without damaging their bodies or egos. They jut out their barrel chests and broaden their shoulders. They carry a big stick. They hope it's enough to force the other guy to back down. "You talkin' to me?" It's a tiny growl, a flick of the tail, a stalling tactic so he can size the other guy up. Which means exactly what it says: He checks out the *size* of his opponent to decide whether it's best to fight or flee.

After considering all the factors—who's watching (if their woman is there, they have to fight and win; if the manager's there, they can start fighting and hope he'll stop it), how old, strong, drunk, or desperate the other guy is—he either stands his ground or puts down the pool cue as a sign of submission. If the challenger is strong enough or stupid enough to take the next step, he says, "Yeah, I'm talkin' to you. I *said* you play pool like a *girl.*" When the challenger does this, he forces a confrontation by saying, "I'm the *man* [ahem]—you're weaker than me, and I'm going to prove it in front of everybody and rub your nose in it." At this point, it's become a matter of manhood. And for a man, that's the same as saying it's become a matter of survival.

It's not exactly that guys *like* to fight, but men who let other men push them around are wimps, sissies—*girls. Real* men—the most powerful, most respected, most feared and revered Alpha males in the pack—don't ever back down. They step outside, they stand up and fight.

Understanding men and conflict—why men lock horns—is understanding all about male *fear.* Men fear appearing unmanly, and most human males define "unmanly" as feeling vulnerable, passive, or hurt. They're basically fearful of any of your random, garden-variety emotions, though exceptions are made for anger, envy, gluttony, sloth, pride, lust, and avarice. (Those puppies sound familiar?)

The instant a man becomes aware of the *other* "deadly" (to him) feelings, he is likely to freak out and lash out, terrified that the world, his woman, his dad, mom, son, daughter, boss, dog, *self* will see the horrible truth: He's not as tough as he pretends to be.

Human male conflict is about control, territory, and status. It's about annihilating the enemy so he, she, they, it won't dare question his authority again. It's about protecting his turf, covering his butt, guarding the family jewels. Men in conflict are afraid of losing power, control, face, self. Power is crucial to gaining and maintaining status in the pack, so any means necessary is justified.

Look, it's not easy being a guy. Most men have internalized the notion that the pressure's always on, from nursery school (boys don't cry) to hunting, fishing, taking care of Mom (being the little man) to high-school sports (Dad's presence at football games) to dating (he asks, he pays, she rejects), to getting into the right school, frat, neighborhood, or meeting the right contacts, mentor, wife, and having successful sons—where it starts all over again. Not only do they have to provide fabulously for their families, they have to protect them, defend them, reassure them, and never let anyone see them sweat while they do it. If a man's not married, he feels he has to have a great job, an even greater salary, a full head of hair, a hot bod, a hot rod, and a sensitive side (but never mushy, sappy, weepy, wimpy, or soft). All without ever asking for directions!

Men have been taught that showing most emotions is a very dangerous lapse since emotions (those deadly ones) are considered toxic to society or toxic to self (the "girl" *thang*). And the most dangerous emotion of all is *fear.* Imagine a husband waking his wife up in the middle of the night in a panic because he heard a noise. "Honey, take the baseball bat and go see who's downstairs," he whispers, choking back the tears, clutching the comforter to his chest. Most men (and most women) would find his

JUNGLE GEMS

Understanding men and conflict means accepting these basic male notions:

- ✦ *Men have been taught that it's dangerous to show or feel fear.*
- ✦ *Fear feels out of control.*
- ✦ *Fearful guys are sissies.*
- ✦ *Sissies are shunned from the pack.*
- ✦ *"Manly" pack members bravely stand up and fight (even when they secretly feel afraid).*
- ✦ *The bravest warriors obliterate the enemy.*
- ✦ *At the first sign of conflict, "real" men regain control by destroying the enemy or refusing to divulge any info (ammo) the enemy can use to destroy them or making any noise the enemy can use to identify their position. And, don'cha know, honey chile, everybody is a potential enemy.*

behavior cowardly, to say the least. But a guy would have to be a lunatic *not* to be afraid. Of course he's scared when something goes bump in the night. His heart is racing, his palms sweating. Yet he grabs the bat and the flashlight and tiptoes downstairs to defend his turf. He performs the way men in our society have been taught, conditioned, and reinforced to perform. He acts like a *man.*

Let's look at that phrase for a moment: *He acts like a man.* It's not enough that he *is* a man, with a penis and XY chromosomes and male pattern baldness, he must also *act* like a man to be perceived as one. In our culture, this means acting brave, stoical, aggressive, impenetrable, confident, competent, and, most of all, fearless. It's almost irrelevant how a man *really* feels. If he acts "manly," society accepts him, women have sex with him, bosses pay him handsomely, and his competitors—other males—back off.

Jane, it's possible as a woman to lift some of the burden off your man's shoulders by reaffirming his value as a *person* (not just a penis or a paycheck), not asking him to do all the scary stuff, going downstairs with him and learning how to swing a bat. If you're a bit stronger, without making him feel that he *can't* do it (try making him feel that you'd like to be a bit more "like" him), he can feel flattered, not threatened. He'll feel like a mentor instead of a "boy" who is mothered and smothered. Pick areas that he doesn't like or doesn't feel are crucial. Heck, take out the garbage, learn to work on the car, put up your own bookcases, and praise him lavishly for his soufflé, tidiness, or ability to calm the kids. We're talking partnership, not competition. Ask him what he thinks rather than telling him what to do.

Animal Instincts

MALE ANIMALS—human and not—"posture" a lot. In the male animal world, as in the human male animal world, aggression is mostly for show. Male animals often snarl and bare their fangs and lunge at one another, but they rarely (that's a relative term) seriously fight and injure one another. Nature set it up that way because it's simply too deadly to the species for it to be otherwise. Instead of allowing unbridled aggression, nature gave animals a way to mark territories, define status, and indicate to one another who rules the roost without anyone having to bleed. Still, nature also gave male animals—and male humans—a competitive nature, so they're constantly testing the boundaries, challenging status, and trying to prove themselves to one another.

In the animal kingdom, there are lots of nonphysical ways to "lock horns." In other words, male animals can "fight" without touching one another. They do this by displaying the aggressive symbols each animal has learned to interpret. Wolves curl their upper lips and plaster their ears to their heads, stags bellow (the longest, loudest wail is usually produced by the biggest, strongest deer), male tree frogs croak out fighting calls that can last more than ten minutes, cats arch their backs, and baboons give one another the evil eye.

These signals are all signs of dominance, status, territorial superiority. Usually they do the trick. Submissive wolves take one look at an Alpha male's fangs and bare their necks, bellies, and genitals. They literally roll over and play dead, because that's exactly what they'd be if the Alpha male chose to attack.

When a young, arrogant upstart does challenge the Alpha male, the stakes get higher. The growling becomes more intense, the *gums* show as well as the teeth, there's a little drooling going on in anticipation of the kill, and the Alpha gets ready to attack. Ideally, that's enough to end the coup. If it isn't, the Alpha male is always ready to go the distance. He has to. Even if he's faced with a younger, stronger opponent, it's a matter of honor, of saving face, of being a male worthy of respect.

Alpha males who win the fight win the right to keep their treasured spot on the top of the heap. They get to keep the best girl, have the best sex, and fill up on the best food first. Alphas who *lose* the fight lose a lot. They are forced to slink off with their tails between their legs and watch younger, stronger males take over. They may even be banished from the pack—forced to try to survive on their own, often a nearly impossible task.

Niccolò Machiavelli, that connoisseur of human power, suggested that pretenders to the throne or powerful generals (and their minions) should be killed or banished so as not to threaten the stability of the state since they are able to attract loyal followers of their own. Who needs to feel like a temporary resident of the master bedroom in your own house, knowing a sexy young stud is waiting in the guest room to warm the sheets in your bed? *Ouch.* No wonder male animals—and human male animals—fight so ferociously when forced into a corner. Successfully resolving conflict is how they survive.

WILD THINGS

Q. All *male animals exhibit aggressive, dominant behavior.*

   a. True

   b. False

A. *False.* Though most male animals clash over mating and territorial rights, male bonobos, commonly called "pygmy chimpanzees," live in peaceful, nonviolent groups based on loving and sharing. In fact, bonobos form social bonds through sex, not war. They share partners, territory, and status . . . and 98 percent of their DNA with humans. Interestingly, the bonobo society is run by *females*, who are dominant over the males, but assert their dominance with such loving care and mild manners, there appears to be equality among the sexes. And even though the females are dominant, the males accept it and are as peaceful as the girls. Perhaps having lots of sex is the answer to calm male conflict. Hey, it's worth a try.

Q. *When two male zebras fight for control of a harem, often the most successful attribute is:*
  a. Size.
  b. Determination.
  c. Agility.

A. *Agility.* Size *doesn't* matter as much when it comes to dominant stallions. Status in the zebra herd is based mostly on age and how long the male zebra has been hanging around. Agility is often a lifesaver more than strength since zebras have to outmaneuver predators to survive. So when two stallions go at it for control of the girls, the most fleet-footed male wins. As with humans, nature—and women—favors animals who've adapted to their environment and done whatever they had to do (learn how to use computers, invest in the stock market, program the VCR) to make it in the world as it exists today.

Boys to Men

HUMAN CONFLICT resolution is taught in childhood. The way a parent reacts to a kid hitting a sibling or a playmate influences the way an adult handles conflicts in life. That's why spanking a kid makes no sense as a punishment for aggressive behavior. Think about it: A parent striking a child while saying, "We don't hit!" is really dumb!

Kids are constantly being frustrated by rules, parents, teachers, older kids. Because boys are seen to be more aggressive and more potentially dangerous than girls, they are allowed more physical freedom to roam, but less interpersonal acting out. Almost from birth, boys are being *controlled*. Girls learn to quietly play Barbies in their bedroom; boys swing from the chandelier. (I actually was threatened with expulsion from sixth grade because I was on the boys' side of the playground playing tetherball!) Think about it: Traditional "girl" games are hopscotch, jump rope, jacks, dolls—stuff that doesn't move very far or very fast. "Boy" games are kickball, tag, touch football, soccer—games that get boys out of the house and on the move.

While it's true that boys tend to be more active than little girls, the question remains: Is it nature or nurture? Are boys born aggressive, or are they taught to express themselves physically, then learn how to constantly control their activity? Does testosterone (men have about ten times more than women) cause aggression, or does aggressive behavior cause testosterone levels to go up? What we're really talking about is a chicken-or-an-egg thing. Which comes first?

What we do know is this: Males prisoners with the highest testosterone levels tend to have the most violent rap sheets. A study of male grad students, however, found that testosterone levels were also likely to rise when students did well and achieved a higher level of status. Testosterone levels go up in male athletes who win their event, and in male spectators who watch their team win. So, when it comes to males and their hormones, the latest research indicates that what we're really talking about is *dominance*, not merely aggression. Boys who learn to satisfy their need for dominance in a positive way don't need to prove themselves with negative aggression.

Interesting, yes? This means that parents of little boys must figure out ways to positively channel their sons' need for dominance. Instead of trying to control, quash, or squash a boy's assertive behavior—and creating a frustrated, angry kid in the process—parents need to learn ways to defuse the frustration, give their sons a sense of control over their own lives (without losing control over their child's life), and let them be the status-seeking, territorial, testosterone-filled animals they are. Parents can do this by letting sons (and daughters) *choose* between alternatives: taking a moment to think of a nonviolent way to handle the situation or *talking* about their feelings (all without letting their children hurt anyone). If boys learn that the only way of dealing with their frustration is by acting out or falling silent, half of our species will be men who are either violent or blowing out their aortas with unexpressed anger.

Raising happy, healthy boys means showing them alternatives to violence. Understand that anger is a feeling; aggression is a behavior. It's okay to *feel* angry, but it's not okay to act out violently. Boys who are angry are frustrated. They feel powerless and out of control. Instead of making them feel more powerless by attempting to control their reaction by sending them to their room, sitting them in a corner, forcing a time-out, parents can say, "Tell me what you want."

"Tell me what you want" is a simple yet powerful tool. It converts physicality into words, an unmanageable feeling into a manageable statement. Parents with kids who act out need to stop the behavior, ask the kids to take a deep breath and a few moments to think about what they want. Say, "As soon as you're ready, tell me what you want." Then learn to listen. If a child says, "I want to clobber my sister," a parent can say, "Okay, everybody feels angry at their sister sometimes. Why do you want to clobber her? How did she make you feel? If you didn't clobber her, how else could you let her know that you're upset?" When a parent waits for the answers, the *child's* answers, the child learns to identify alternatives on his own.

Good parenting requires more time than most parents feel they have today. But children won't see alternatives until their parents do. If women view talking to their sons as emasculating them, or sending them to their rooms as acceptable punishment, it will simply continue the cycle of teaching boys to grow into men who can't communicate.

Ever wonder why so many men walk away when arguing with a woman? Their moms probably sent them to their rooms as boys when their behavior got out of control. They learned early on that sitting alone in silence is how you deal with a conflict between males and females.

Not only is sending a boy to his room a bad idea because it teaches him *not* to communicate, it also reinforces his negative behavior. Sending a boy to his room is essentially saying that he doesn't have to deal with anybody. Which is what makes him happiest. It's saying, "Your sister is making you crazy, your mother's demands are emasculating you, but when you get nasty, your mother will get out of your face and give you space, silence, solitude."

In short, too many males (for too many years) have learned that bad behavior leads to peace and quiet. (Not to mention that most kids' rooms look like Disneyland anyway. Even if the kid isn't playing, why use the same room for punishment that should be used to feel safe enough to relax in and go to sleep in nightly?)

Kids who act out are saying, "This situation feels uncomfortable for me. Anything is better than what I'm feeling." Which is why kids who have a hard time at school are often the class clowns. Disruption feels good because it feels so awful to sit there in discomfort. Doing something "bad" feels better than living in a chronic state of tension. The status quo sucks, so even being punished feels better. At least this way they are in control—they brought punishment on themselves and can deal with a real event, the punishment, better than they can deal with free-floating anxiety. But punishing the aggression is really just punishing the symptom. Parents, teachers, and caretakers need to take the time to ask, "What do you want?" then take even more time to listen to the answer.

HIStory

MEN HAVE BEEN locking horns with one another from the beginning of time. Human history is the history of male conflict and territorialism: You've got it, I want it, I'm going to fight you for it. Warrior kings rose out of the chaos in Mesopotamia around 3500 B.C. to lead factions who fought for control of the first civilization, Sumer. The first Chinese dynasty, the Shang, ruled with a cadre of warrior landlords who violently snatched land from the peasants. Before the Babylonian warrior king Hammurabi (himself a brawler) established the first code of law around 1750 B.C., vendetta and revenge was the way men routinely settled disputes.

Successful warriors are revered. I mean, if it wasn't for Achilles' heel, he'd probably still be fighting. Bravery in battle entitled you to have "the Great" follow your name (Alexander, Peter, and, okay, *one* woman, Catherine, but she was known more for *construction* than *destruction*). Go to a museum and look at early art— pottery drawings and murals often depict muscled men fighting with one another. If men didn't have battles to dream up and plan and fight and sweat in and win, they'd probably just twiddle their thumbs till one of 'em said, "I can twiddle faster than you." We know where that would lead soon enough—the side of a vase or mosaic.

War itself has historically been a way for men to define themselves as men. The term *coward* is rarely used to describe a *woman*. In war, men are asked to place a lesser value on their own lives than on that of the group. The *corps* is what's important. Look at the Marine Corps motto: Unit, Corps, God, Country. The individual is lost entirely. Natural, human feelings and needs (fear, self-preservation) are obliterated for the good of the group. Which is why the military is such a *male*-oriented organization. Men are used to squashing their feelings and needs (fear, closeness) in order to appear brave.

Try to do this to most women and you'll hear them say, "What are you talking about? If my life doesn't mean anything, then I cease to exist. What good is that?" Even when women die for their children, they die *protecting* their kids, not for the greater good of their family lives. To women, who are accustomed to expressing their needs and verbally bonding with one another, war makes precious little sense. Until recently, women didn't have to even pretend to be brave. They'd ask instead, "Can't we all just get along? Why must you kill our sons?" One of the great examples of women's response to men's combative nature can be seen in Aristophanes' play *Lysistrata*, where the women get creative and strike for peace by refusing to have sex with men who fight.

The point is, men have always felt the need to prove themselves, increase their status, and expand their territories by any means necessary. It's no accident, then, that in the absence of war, men need to channel their aggressive energy elsewhere.

Men and Conflict

ODERN MALES in modern *civilized* society deal with their aggressive impulses in three major ways: silence, violence, and revenge. Hmmmm . . . doesn't sound that different from the way it was in Mesopotamia, does it? The difference is, warrior kings are now angry guys in speeding SUVs, explosive husbands, gang members, and disgruntled postal workers. The feelings of frustration, powerlessness, and territorialism are the same; we've simply updated the methods of expression.

The "silent treatment" is the ultimate form of *passive* aggression. It's a way to manipulate and control the uncomfortable situation. Men who shut down, tune out, and turn off in the face of conflict are saying, "I'm going to shut *you* up by not acknowledging your presence." The silent treatment is really a statement of fear. Strong, silent types have learned that talking their way through a conflict is dangerous. When you talk, you're revealing information the enemy can use against you. You're *aiding* the enemy.

Trying to win a talking fight is a losing battle, so they clam up in an attempt to quiet their opponent, too. They try to end the conflict by not participating in it. Of course, all it does is anger the other side even more.

Jane, I know his silence drives you nuts, but understand, number one, that men are raised to be physically oriented more than verbally expressive. This not only means that he's less likely to talk about his feelings than you are, it also means he's tuned in to body language. It's the "Actions speak louder than words" phenomenon. So even if you've learned not to verbally hound him when the two of you disagree, it's also important to give him *phys-*

ical space as well. Fuming and silently glaring at him from across the room is, to him, almost the same as getting in his face and having a screaming hissy fit. Just as you think the "right" way to argue is to talk things out (even if the "talk" is heated), he thinks the best way to cope with conflict is to crawl into the safety of his shell (room, office, car, television set, best friend's house) until he gathers his thoughts and calms down.

Number two, men have learned that women really *don't* want to hear what they have to say when they're angry. You say to him, "Tell me how you feel!" but we both know you want him to say that he loves you, is sorry he's such a jerk, and will never hurt you ever again. What a guy's probably *really* feeling is, "Get out of my face," "Can we wrap this up before the kickoff?" or "Does this mean I'm not going to get sex tonight?" Men feel that women use talk to ensnare them. Women are more experienced at wordplay than men are, so guys don't want to play at all. Your man knows that you're going to nail him the first time he says something you don't want to hear. Why look foolish? It's easier and safer for him to shut down.

The next time he does go mute, do yourself a favor (and stun the daylights out of him) by saying, "We don't have to talk about this right now." Then turn around and walk away. Do something positive and physical for yourself. Movement is a great tension releaser. Put on your sneakers and take a walk in the park, take a bubble bath, jump a rope. Remove yourself from the temptation to *force* your style of conflict resolution on him. Because that's really what it is: two different *styles* of communicating. Labeling one good and one bad doesn't do anybody any good. Give him time and space to feel less threatened, more in control, less like a little boy who got caught doing something bad, and he'll probably be so grateful he'll come to you and apologize. If he doesn't, quietly schedule a "meeting" at which to discuss the problem. That way, you give him structure (he won't feel ambushed) and time to shore up his feelings of masculinity again.

Tarzan, you're a man and your woman wants to sit down and talk whenever you want to stand and run. Understanding that *both* of you are responding to your animal nature may make it a bit easier to accept. Women view conversation as the path to intimacy, whereas you'll open up at the *end* of the road . . . if at all. That's okay. You don't have to become somebody you're not. That never works for anybody. What might work better when it comes to resolving conflict is to look at your woman's behavior in a slightly different light. While it may feel as though she's trying to trap you with her words, or force you to feel sorry when you really just feel annoyed, most of the time women feel terribly frightened in a conflict with their men. Her relationship with you is probably the most important relationship in her life. That scares the dickens out of her, and maybe you, too. The point is, a conflict with you can quickly escalate in her mind to abandonment, loss of love and security . . . all the things she holds near and dear. When women feel afraid, they often try to *talk* their way out of it, which is probably part of what she's doing when she's blabbing on and on with you, or they try to keep you close by ensnaring you in their words. Without being aware of it, she's probably saying to you, "I'm scared, I love you, I don't want to lose you, please don't be mad at me." What often comes out, however, is something like this: "You're so inconsiderate, you never listen, you just don't get it, I'm mad as hell at you."

What women really want when arguing with their men is *reassurance.* They want to know that you will be there to work things out. Telling her, "I love you. Things feel awful right now, but everything's going to be okay," will not only calm her, it'll quiet her down, too. When you protect her and console her (even when you're feeling miffed at her), her need to verbally build a bridge between the two of you diminishes. She can exhale and let go and say, "Phew! We're going to work things out. I can relax now."

Understanding that a relationship is more like a seed than a flower (growing, not already grown) will help you redefine each new conflict as, not a petal falling off the rose, but a bit of fertilizer. It feels like manure right now, but it's necessary for the most vibrant blossom. Our lives and relationships are all works in progress. *Nobody* likes to be controlled, and anger must be released to disappear. In fact, a researcher at the Hypertension Center of New York Presbyterian Hospital, Samuel J. Mann, M.D., found that people who repress their emotions are more than three times as likely to develop hypertension as those who don't.

Genetics aside, and the oral contraceptive aside, hypertension is much more a male disease than a female one (17 percent of white women aged thirty-five to forty-five compared to 26 percent of white men the same age; among blacks thirty-five to forty-five, it's 37 percent women compared to 44 percent men). Facing feelings head-on can lower high blood pressure enough that medication may be discontinued. Frustration and anger are like mold: They spread and grow in dark, damp places but shrivel up and die when exposed to light and air.

Explosion, temper, violence are often male responses to frustration and aggression. They rage, they holler, they get in the car and tailgate other drivers and scare the daylights out of everybody on the road. Explosive anger is a preemptive strike. It's a Scud missile (a *stud* missile?); it's saying, "I'm going to clobber you before you clobber me." Men who explode in a rage are saying,

"You're trying to control me, you're being my mom, you're telling me what to do, I can't deal with it, so how can I disrupt the situation? I'll holler." And guess what? It usually works.

An explosion stops the initial conflict in its tracks. The argument is no longer about what's bugging someone, it's about the raging guy's *reaction*. It becomes a discussion about calming down, overreacting, chilling out. The explosive male has shifted the power—now *he's* in control. Disruption is always a form of control. An explosion shifts the focus away from the feelings stirred up by the initial conflict (very scary) to actively taking control over what's going on (much more comfortable). In the long and short run, explosive anger is a way of never really dealing with conflict at all.

Explosive anger on the road—road rage—is a uniquely modern way some people react to frustration and feeling out of control. "Aggressive driving" has been named by the United States government as one of the most serious transportation problems we have today. The majority of aggressive drivers are men aged eighteen to twenty-six. It's amazing how quickly mild-mannered guys can turn into raging lunatics on the road. A male friend of mine—a kind, well-educated, high-placed executive—told me about an incident that happened to him on the road. He was cut off by a guy in traffic who then turned into his driveway. My friend— I'll call him Ted—tooted his horn as he passed the driveway, "just to let him know he didn't get away with it." The guy then threw his car into reverse and backed *out* of the driveway, racing to catch up to Ted's car. He did, aggressively hanging on his bumper until he had the opportunity to change lanes, zoom ahead of Ted's car, then swerve in front of him to cut him off again. Now, knowing that Ted is a gun enthusiast, I said, "You didn't happen to have a gun in your glove compartment, did you?" Ted's eyes lit up and he said,

"You were reading my mind. I really wish I'd had a gun or a tire iron to brandish at the guy!"

I'm talking intelligent, major executive, and he wishes he'd had a *gun* to threaten some guy who cut him off? Mighty scary stuff. Not only that, but Ted admitted that the whole incident has haunted him ever since it happened. Not because his animalistic nature overrode his human intelligence, but because he felt "less of a man because he didn't do anything." In Ted's mind, a "real" man would have accepted the other guy's challenge and fought to the finish. Which says a lot about men and conflict—it's not enough to defend themselves, they must *annihilate* the enemy. Real men don't just fight fire with fire, they drop the atom bomb. Which is what road rage really is, attacking a slight (cutting you off, giving the finger, tailgating, driving too slow) with a deadly weapon, attempting to regain control by potentially losing control of your car.

Jane, as long as your guy is only hollering, don't freak out, wait him out, let him cool off, don't leave the room, don't try to out yell him, and for heaven's sake, don't laugh unless you simply can't help yourself. Wait till he's through, then sweetly ask, "Feel better?" He'll likely, rather abashedly, say, "Yes." Then you can calmly say, "Okay, now let's figure out what we want to do here. What do you think? Then I'll tell you my idea and see what you think about that." However, all bets are off if there's even a hint of physical violence. Then you've got to leave for both of your sakes.

The third way some guys express aggression is through revenge, which is related to road rage, but not as incendiary. Revenge is more of a *slow* burn. It's the "Don't get mad, get even" philosophy of life. It's why guys rarely quit a job in a huff the way women do. Instead, they plot sabotage, biding their time until they can really *get* the boss. Men are much more likely to steal files, go to a competitor, plant a computer virus. Until they're ready to kill, men are much more apt to suck up, bare their necks, kiss butt. The male competitive nature won't allow them to take on the boss until they're prepared to take him *down*. What this creates is obsession, simmering anger, and blown aortas. Guys will say it's a matter of principle; really, it's a matter of manhood. The guy who backs down, the one who blinks first, feels as though he's sacrificing his manhood to a stronger, smarter, sexier, fitter Alpha male. The stakes are so high, which is why men in conflict often feel as if even the smallest skirmishes are nuclear *war*.

Jane and Tarzan: As parents, you'll only be able to raise nonviolent boys who become nonviolent men by examining your own behavior first. Kids study their parents to learn how to behave. If you bang the steering wheel in anger, or zoom up someone's tailpipe each time another driver makes a dumb move on the road, your son will learn that anger in a car is normal. Studies show that parents influence a child's aggression in a number of ways, including rejection (constantly disapproving your child's behavior), punishing physically, not nurturing kids enough (not being aware of their needs and activities, not making the time to truly *listen*), venting your own frustrations inappropriately (hollering, hitting, plotting revenge), and allowing kids to watch too much violence on TV. It's not just that television violence stirs up a boy's testosterone, it's that kids learn *how* to act aggressively by watching TV characters do aggressive things, and constant viewing of violence may weaken a child's natural inhibitions to doing something dangerous or antisocial.

I'm not suggesting you have to be the TV police, but as parents, you do have a responsibility to be more careful. Kids are sponges. The best way to make sure they don't soak up negative behaviors is to make sure there aren't many around. Limit the number of weekly TV hours, let the kids schedule their faves, and try and watch at least *some* with them. Of course, I'm in favor of the "No TV on school nights" rule—that's why VCRs were invented. If you say, "No TV till your homework is done," guess what gets short shrift? You got it—the *homework*.

When your child does get upset and frustrated, say, "Tell me what you want." Then take the time to listen. If you don't have time for a long involvement, it's okay to say, "Look, why don't we agree to stop this. Sounds like you're feeling frustrated, but we just don't have time to talk about it right now. Let's make an appointment to talk about this tonight when you come home, and neither of us will worry between now and then." Or you can say, "Tell me how long you would like to take to think about this, and then tell me when and what you'd like to do about it." Giving them some control over what's going to happen takes away the negative anticipation of "You're going to get it."

Kids learn much more by example than by what parents *say*. The notion of parenting as "Do what I say, not what I do" is not only unproductive, it's destructive. The best way to raise nonviolent boys is to *show* them alternatives to violence in your everyday life.

Working It Out Together

MEN IN CONFLICT with women complain that women never shut up; women in conflict with men complain that men never open up. The quieter he gets, the more frustrated she gets. The more he senses her anger, the tighter his lips clamp down. It's a vicious cycle that keeps conflict alive instead of giving conflict the air and light it needs to dissipate.

Understanding that men are emotionally claustrophobic is crucial when dealing with any type of male/female conflict. Cornering a guy, limiting his movement, issuing an ultimatum are all the emotional equivalent of strapping on a straitjacket. He'll do whatever it takes to squirm free. The human male response to threat is the same as the male animal response: They lash out, attack, annihilate the enemy, go for the throat, kill or be killed. Attempting to intimidate or threaten any male animal is counterproductive. There are simply too many primal instincts firing off alarms all over his body for him to calmly discuss how he feels. When it comes to human male animals, perceived "threats" include the phrases "We need to talk," "What are you thinking?" and "Have a seat." Women who attempt to resolve conflicts with their men this way are going to lose. His body and mind hears, "Fire!" and every muscle springs for the nearest exit.

I'm not suggesting that women wrap themselves in Saran Wrap and purr like a kitten, but the idea is to work out viable strategies that are useful when it comes to resolving conflicts between men and women. Public places, time limits, a walk in the park (that shoulder-to-shoulder thing again), less talk, more space all work well. Trapping him guarantees he'll gnaw his own foot off to get out.

Jane, Tarzan—maybe both of you can decide *not* to keep score. Ask each other, "How can we end this conflict now, so we can move on, find something else to argue about, go eat, make love, play with the kids, find ice cream?" If nothing ever gets resolved—the "you always, you never" jazz—find a marriage counselor or a lawyer.

QUANTUM

MEN

Admit feeling fearful; no one else has to know.

Attach the symptoms of your fear to something specific (my heart's beating too fast) so you avoid free-floating anxiety.

Figure out what triggers your fear (I came home to an empty house).

Figure out what you're *really* afraid of. Facing it keeps you from being steamrollered by those feelings.

Understand that most acts of "bravery" require turning off your survival instinct—calculate the cost/benefit ratio before you act.

Winning and losing aren't the only choices. Remember you *can* lose battles and win wars.

WOMEN

Just because he *has* to win doesn't mean you have to lose.

Reduce the appearance of conflict by communicating more and arguing less.

Ask a man, "If you were me, what would you do?"

Explore your own independence and strength—you don't always need help.

Don't use sex as a weapon. Withholding affection isn't fighting fair. Fighting fair means fighting *less*.

Never say, "If you loved me, you'd know." Tell him.

LEAPS

Six

Mating

Men and Sex

MALE JACKDAWS MATE at age one and remain faithful to their mates for the rest of their long lives—up to sixty-five years. Australian broad-footed marsupial male mice die after breeding only once. Petite male elephant seals pretend to be girls and sneak into the harem to mate, snakes literally tie themselves up in knots, birds do it in trees, bees do it with a queen, and the studliest male peacocks are all eyes. The point is, in any corner of the male animal world, it's *all* about sex.

Male animals sniff out a receptive female, check out the equipment, and go to town. They not only live for sex, their whole existence is defined by how successfully they can impregnate.

Sex is the most primitive of the primal instincts. It's survival. Male animals have adapted in every conceivable way to get the girl—courtship dances, mating rituals, aphrodisiac secretions, bobbing, weaving, grooming, bearing gifts, pinning her down in the jaws of death. Whatever works. But getting the girl is no simple matter.

Other males may get in the way because horny males are ready to rumble—partly because their testosterone is all revved up and they're feeling, well, *testy*, and partly because the mating season is short and their desire is long, and partly because females are picky and guys have to prove that they have the best sperm on the market. Which usually comes from the biggest, toughest, *manliest* males, who can beat the daylights out of other males. (Hey, moms-to-be want to make sure their offspring can hack it in the dog-eat-dog world.) A recent Swedish study shows that ovulating women prefer brawny guys over their more sensitive counterparts who appeal to them at other, less fertile times in their cycles. Talk about your throw-back syndrome!

Some female animals choose the *brightest* males around. I'm not talking *smarts*, but males with flashy, vibrant show-off colors: the Liberaces of the animal kingdom. These pretty boys are hot stuff. Experiments show that females prefer males who stimulate *all* their senses. They're also attracted to males who already have females. (Hmmmm . . . I don't have to worry if he's attractive—he's already gotten someone's Good Housekeeping Seal of Approval.)

So sexual selection is a complex dance with a very simple goal: mating . . . by any means necessary. The male is the pursuer; the female lets him know when it's time to pursue. He's revving his engines; she gives him the the stoplight, a bit of caution, or go, go, go! Millions of sperm are called; few are chosen. And when it's (quickly) over, the male goes back to hanging with his buddies, and the bare-pawed and pregnant female waddles away to prepare to create a home for the kids.

The Human Animal

I F MALE ANIMAL sexuality is all about survival, human male sexuality is about *control*, which *feels* like survival. It's about both gaining and losing control of self, about status, manhood. Sex is exhilarating and terrifying. And even though ballads and novels would have us believe that sex between a man and a woman is the only time our souls can merge, the aftermath can also be the loneliest experience a couple can have together because they both view sexuality so differently.

Once we get past "this part goes in that part," human sexuality is interpretation, communication, and integration. And when it comes to sexual communication, most men are convinced that women lie to them about sex. Or let's just say they are less than trustworthy and honest. Okay, to start with, I am talking "faking it," which includes the "Yeah, I had an orgasm" lie and the "Ooooh, baby, baby, you're the best [first, only]" lie. But the truly *big* sexual lie is the one that the guys fear. That's the lie a woman tells when before, during, or after sex, she asks the guy to "tell me how you feel." Most guys have found out the hard way that she's not looking for an honest answer. All she really wants to hear is "I love you, you're gorgeous, I feel close to you, I'll never leave you." She *doesn't* want to hear what he's *really* thinking, especially if it's along the lines of "I wonder if I can get this finished before the first pitch."

There's a lot women really *don't* want to hear when they say, "Tell me what you want" or "Tell me how you feel." If he's really fantasizing about her best friend (or *his* best friend) or comparing the just-completed behavior with masturbating in the shower or wondering whether she'd look better ten pounds lighter, she'd rather he kept it to himself. And admit it, Jane, do you really want to hear that your man is afraid, that he's growing older and his penis doesn't always do what he wants it to do? Do you really want to hear that he fears that you care more about the kids than about him, and wonders if you dream of having sex with somebody else because you sure don't seem to want sex with him?

Be careful what you ask for in the truth department. When both of you are naked physically as well as emotionally, a little "truth" goes a long way. So do women really want to hear this kind of "truth"? No. When a woman asks a man to tell her how he feels sexually, she is actually asking to be reassured that she is pretty, has a good body, is beloved, worth a commitment, experienced enough to turn him on (but not too experienced to turn him off), and is the only, best, sexiest lover in his life. Plus, she wants to hear that she erases the memory of any other female.

Jane, if that's what you want, for heaven's sake, ask for it! Don't kid yourself (and him) that you really want to hear what he's thinking. Of if you do, no fair crying, whining, or storming out of bed if you hear something you don't really like.

Even if your man knows what to say to reassure you, he probably won't have much *more* to say. Expecting his flattery to be a bridge to deeper thoughts is unrealistic because most men don't even begin to understand their own sexuality, which further compounds this sexual communication gridlock or lockjaw. They instinctively keep themselves in the dark, fearing that delving too deeply into the whys and wherefores will overburden the "little guy's" head and literally leave *both* heads exhausted and impotent.

When I say that men don't think about sex, I'm not talking about *fantasizing* about it. Men's fantasies are about always winning in the end, about being in charge and having every actress (or actor, or actress and actor) do exactly as directed without question, discussion, or judgment. *Thinking* is different. It's analytical by its very definition. Figuring out the whys and wherefores, *thinking* about sex while they're doing it, is the equivalent of doing multiplication tables. It's getting out of the feeling, the moment, and getting into the "big head." It's what guys do when they want to disrupt nature or prolong an erection, distract themselves from premature or inappropriate arousal in order to stop the flow, not stem the tide. Disrupting nature is fine when you're fifteen and life is seen through a spermy green haze, but when you're thirty or forty or fifty, Mother Nature (we won't even go *there*) can be fickle, spiteful, unpredictable, and entirely whimsical.

And so guys figure it's best to leave well enough alone and hope for the best. For them, sex is about *un*thinking. It's about diving in. Thinking too much causes impotence, and impotence feels unmanly. Feeling unmanly feels like a girl, and feeling like a girl feels awful. So most guys like it best when sex is a physical thing—when it's all about the *little* head and the big head is disengaged. *En*gagement is connection (the engagement ring announces to everybody, "Hands off, she's *mine*"). *Dis*engagement is separation. In the case of male sexuality, it's *mental* separation so the physical sensations can take over. It's a male form of tunnel vision (and we know which tunnel he's focused on). "No thinking, thank you. Just *feeling*, please." The difference between the male and female approach to *thinking* about sex would be ironic if it weren't so perverse. The same thing that is a turnoff for men—being analytical, thinking play by play—is a turn-on for women. Planning it, dissecting every movement and moment, makes *her* feel secure and safe, which allows her to be reassured enough—physically and emotionally—to literally put herself in his hands and let loose enough to *wham!* have an orgasm and then stay awake to do the slo-mo replay.

A woman saying, "What could you have been thinking when you tried that maneuver?!" is right on the money. He wasn't thinking. Thinking is often the last thing a guy is looking forward to when he contemplates sex. Physical *feelings* are what he's after, and since men are given so little opportunity or permission to feel *anything*, you can understand the incredible, well, *seduction* of male sex as disengaged from emotions or other parts of a guy's psyche and personality. It's why guys like porn, it's why guys go to prostitutes, strip joints, it's why men can have sex with women without knowing their name. Ultimately, it's why men and women are often on two different tracks sharing the same bed.

A man, Edmund, forty-three, called my program to ask why his wife refused sex until he helped out around the house. "What's one thing got to do with the other?" he said. I asked him if he worked. He said, yeah, he was the manager of a retail store. So I said, "Ed, if you have an employee who is always late, often dog-ging it, appears not to care very much unless it's payday, you gonna give him a Christmas bonus? A promotion? You gonna take him out to lunch? No, you're gonna feel ripped off. You may have to do the minimum amount so you don't get slapped with a discrimi-nation suit, but you're not going to put yourself out. That's what your wife is doing—*not* putting herself out, not giving you a bonus, until you become a team player."

He replied, "Yeah, but it's *sex.*" Ed—it's not that she doesn't like sex, but it's a lot harder for most women to disengage their feelings from themselves. Partially, it's biological—sex is an inva-sion of her body space. She has to feel safe in order to relax enough for penetration to occur. She may not have to feel "in love," but she has to feel *unthreatened,* which translates into feeling cherished, feeling important, *not* feeling used or abused. Sex for men is about feeling aroused. A woman has to be relaxed to be aroused. Anger or tension is the enemy of relaxation. When some-one is angry, as Ed's wife obviously is, adrenaline starts pumping and the fight-or-flight response is activated. Exactly the opposite of what a woman needs to feel sexual. Women must, literally, be open to receiving another person inside her body. She has to trust and feel secure. By definition, sex for a woman is vulnerability, often being relatively helpless with somebody who is usually big-ger and stronger. And it's not only physical vulnerability at stake. Biologically, sociologically, and psychologically she may also feel vulnerable. She can get pregnant, besmirched, labeled a "slut." Male vulnerability is primarily genital: His sexual apparatus is external, and while he may be fearful that his genitals will be found lacking, he's still the invad*er* instead of the invad*ee*. A guy who sleeps around is a stud, and no man will ever get pregnant. Again, for a woman to feel comfortable sexually, she has to feel safe. She has to feel cherished. Otherwise she's just a receptacle.

Ed's wife feels cherished when he helps around the house. She feels *safe.* He's saying to her, "I revere you, I won't leave you, I won't treat you like my servant. You're not alone; I'm right beside you." He's thinking, "It's only a dirty dish." She's thinking, "He really does love me." It's not a trade-off—you do the dishes, I'll roll over for you. It's feeling like she *matters* to him. That's what turns a woman on.

Men, on the other hand, can be turned on by almost any-thing: a flash of thigh, long silky hair, the thought of a nooner. Since sex is primarily a physical event, a sudden breeze can send guys straight to the bedroom. Men know this and women know this. Only very young, or much older, women are flattered by an erection. Young women don't realize that an erection isn't neces-sarily a personal statement about how much she turns him on, one way or the other; older women understand that older men have a more difficult time getting an erection, so they feel good when he does. But the notion of "giving" a man an erection is false at its core. If men could be *given* erections, Viagra wouldn't be the hottest-selling drug in America. And trust me, no man would ever choose to be impotent.

Guys are painfully aware that erections are often beyond their control. Or, at any moment, the "little" head will develop a mind of its own. As sophisticated as many people are about sexual stimulation and partner-pleasing, the erect penis is still the symbol of manhood and virility. Don't take my word for it, just look at the language! Synonyms for *erect* are *elevated, firm*, and *upstanding*. Synonyms for *flaccid* are *debilitated, enfeebled,* and *nerveless*. Even the word *testicle* comes from the Latin *testis*, meaning "a witness to virility." *Testis* is also the root of the word *testify*: telling the truth, standing up, bearing witness, being a *man*.

Ever wonder why . . .

. . . guys roll over and fall asleep right after sex? Male energy is targeted on the Big Event. Flowers, dinner, sweet nothings whispered in her ear—all steps leading to, *ta da!* EJACULATION. "Making love" for men is foreplay; *ejaculation* is sex. Hence the term *coming,* as in "I have arrived!" After men have "arrived," they can rest. They've *won.* For women, *after* sex is after *glow.* It's where the yummy stuff begins—the cuddling, snuggling, cooing, *closeness.* Women say, "How could he fall asleep when we were feeling so close?!" Men say, "Why does she continue with foreplay when the party's over?"

Jane, if you want more sex, don't assume that every guy is a drooling hound dog, after one thing and one thing only. It simply isn't true. Male and female sex drives are actually quite similar—both men and women have sexual urges and release them through intercourse or masturbation. The sexual differences between men and women center on intimacy issues, not the sex act itself. It's the difference between *feeling* sexy and having sex. What you want to do is create an environment in which your partner feels sexy. If your partner is a woman, that means making her feel cherished and special. If your partner is a man, it means making him feel powerful, in charge, respected, needed.

So what's that mean in terms of behavior? Well, if you're constantly whining for sex and he's not in the mood, or physically not ready, he'll feel inadequate as a partner, a lover, and a man—three decidedly *un*sexy feelings. Letting him know that you love him and want him, then backing off, gives him the chance to feel powerful instead of nagged and humiliated.

Look, I know this sounds a bit Donna Reedish, but the idea is to try what *works*. Forcing somebody onto *your* sexual timetable is not only foolish, it's unproductive and makes everybody feel lousy. The aim is for both of you to feel relaxed and loved, not pressured and pestered.

Once you're having sex, Jane, the best way to have the kind of sex you desire is to *ask* for it. No one is a *born* lover. Great sex is created between two people who want to please each other. If he's not pleasing you, ask him in a gentle, loving way to do what you want him to do. Instructions don't work, requests do. Keep it short and sweet and simple. I know it's difficult to open up, but if you can't communicate verbally, you'll have problems communicating sexually as well.

You might also take turns being each other's love slave—you direct him as to what you like one night and let him be in charge directing you the next night. No potential ouchies allowed, and if you're suggesting something new, go slowly. Everyone likes to feel cherished, trusted, trustworthy, in charge, and taken care of—oh, the variety of possibilities!

Tarzan, if you want more sex, understand that the female sexual response works very differently than yours does. Expecting her to be hot simply because you are will make both of you unhappy. You want more sex? Give her more affection. Often it's as simple as that. Relaxation is crucial. But giving her a back rub just so she'll roll over as soon as you're through will only work once or twice. After that, I guarantee you, she's gonna feel used and you're gonna toss your hands in the air and say, "Women!"

Showing your love *outside* of the bedroom by doing the dishes, picking up the kids, picking up your dirty socks, will work so well that it will astonish you. I once had a caller tell me she got incredibly turned on when she woke up one morning to find the dishwasher emptied and the coffee made.

And, Jane, if you can't get your man to tell you what he wants sexually, try asking him to write it down. Putting it into words isn't always comfortable, so it's important to make any sexual partner feel safe enough to ask for anything. The result may start a fire that surprises you both. But if there's something there that makes you feel a little awkward or embarrassed, it's okay to say so. You don't have to do what you don't want to do. No matter what he says or writes down, though, it's *not* okay to ridicule or judge anybody's sexual desires. If you do, you'll never hear another one again. And since great sex is all about communication, that's the last thing you want to have happen!

You have to understand that sex for most men is a battle for *control*—maintaining control over the uncontrollable (the penis), losing control of the controlled (the mind), and feeling out of control (tingly, heart racing, breathless) most of the time. Which is why guys divorce themselves from their penis. Again, look at the language: Men call their penis their *member, Johnson, third leg, salami.* They refer to their penis as a separate entity—not a part of their body, but a buddy (enemy, evil twin) with a mind of his own. Men don't want to take responsibility for controlling this uncontrollable *being,* so they separate themselves from it. Imagine a woman saying, "My *vagina* got the better of me last night." Not going to happen.

In bed, the male struggle for control and dominance is transferred onto his partner. Consider the missionary position. He's on top, she's pinned down, he controls movement, she's in the most vulnerable pose possible—neck bared, soft underbelly exposed; he's smothering her, she can't escape. And this is the sexual position condoned by the Church! Plus, the missionary position means you're face-to-face. It's forcing the female to *see* and acknowledge the male, the potential father of her offspring. He wants to make sure she has no doubt who Daddy is.

And if you think the missionary position is fraught with emotional peril, common variations are even more challenging, since the dominance factor often increases. Take oral sex, for instance. The male is literally jamming something down a female's throat. He's in her face, keeping her quiet. Male sex is an invasion of body space. It's why homosexuality is so frightening to most men. Particularly with anal sex, not only can a competitor sneak up behind you, he can *enter* you, control you, dominate you. Women who think men are trying to lord it over them in bed have a serious amount of historical and biological precedent. It's undoubtedly the reason why our language uses the same slang words to describe sex and serious aggression.

Tarzan, Jane, you're both having to deal with big changes in the way we all deal with sex and our sexuality. These changes are due to two main factors: increased life expectancy and birth control. Human mating is now more recreation than procreation, which has caused a lot of confusion between the sexes in the past century. In the 1800s families had an average of seven kids; families now average *fewer than* two. Marriages used to literally die before the youngest child was out of the house. Now couples have as much time alone after raising kids as they had during it. Or they never even have kids at all. And this is affecting every part of our relationships—not just our bedroom behavior.

Women have not only become the men they want to marry, they're physically strong enough to beat 'em up, and can function independently of his traditional male "gifts"—money, protection, marriage, everything . . . save his *sperm.* Poor men: Sexually, guys still check out their equipment and want to go to town, but a woman can say, "Maybe later" or "I'm not in the mood" or "Why don't I just go to a sperm bank and get a Yale grad?" Men feel less relevant to women, their kids, their jobs, the very survival of the species—which is a very dangerous feeling when a guy is in bed trying to perform.

As men are feeling less relevant, symbols take on an added emotional weight: who takes out the garbage, nights out with the boys, even *labels.* A divorced woman in her thirties called my program with a dilemma. She had two kids and was about to be married for the second time. "My fiancé wants me to change my name back to my maiden name before the wedding," she said. "And the wedding is in four months!" She told me she wanted to please her husband-to-be but couldn't figure out why it was such a big deal to him. It was clear to me that her fiancé was trying to *revirginize* his bride. He was trying to pretend that he was the first. It seemed silly to go to all that trouble for four months; plus, there's the effect it would have on her kids, who would certainly want to keep their last name. So I suggested she take her fiancé's hand, sit him down, and gently say, "You've got to accept me as I am—a formerly married woman with two kids and an ex." If he can't do that before the wedding, he's sure not going to do it afterward. Women undoubtedly try to remake their mates into the man of their dreams—change his manners, his clothes, his friends, his job, his education, his status. Women tend to see men for their potential— not what they are but what they *might* be or become. Men want their women to return to those stunning days of yesteryear when they were younger, more pliable, more virginal, which is why asking a wife to lose weight, go blond, don't go gray, and dress sexier isn't uncommon. Conversely, a husband is allowed to get gray, heavy, and wrinkly as long as he dresses well and proceeds up the business ladder.

When guys feel powerless, they feel *awful.* Often they'll do anything to literally get back on top. Men who go to prostitutes are often trying to rekindle that sense of biological superiority. Sex with a prostitute is a business transaction, it's nothing personal. The john is in charge. He doesn't have to care about the prostitute, worry about her orgasm or her birth control, respect her, help her with the housework, call her in the morning. He can ask her to do anything in the dark, and not have to face her judgmental (or fearful) eyes in the morning. He can feel safe; there's no witness if his penis doesn't work. She'll *listen,* tell him how manly he is, let him act out his fantasies no matter how scary they seem. For some men, sex with a prostitute lets them reconnect with their animal instincts. It's a *physical* act. It's sniffing out a receptive female, checking out the equipment, and going to town—without all that scary thinking, feeling stuff to muck things up. It's a way for a man who may be feeling an attack of the *irrelevants* to feel important again.

And as long as we're talking important, let's take a quick peek at pornography here. It simultaneously gives a guy the sense that he's in charge—the penis is at full attention—and gives his woman the feeling that she's completely irrelevant. Jane, let's say your guy likes porn. Don't take it *personally!* Women think men watch porn and compare their sex lives to the sex lives they see on the screen or in the magazine. Instant inadequacy. Nobody looks like that in real life! Not to mention, how many women *really* throw themselves at the cable installer (and invite three friends over to do the same)? Porn is not about *you*, it's about visually stimulating your man. The same with strip joints. He doesn't want the dancer to be his wife, he wants to be turned on. He's *not* comparing you to anyone. He's aware of his own arousal and focusing his warm and fuzzy feelings on you. For men, it's a four-step process: (1) I'm aroused. (2) I'm aware of being aroused. (3) I'm looking for some place to use this good stuff. (4) Where's my woman? Because women are both less physiologically dependent on arousal and less accepting of their physical rather than emotional self, they short-circuit the same process and look for *emotional* arousal rather than physical arousal. Men are jump-started physically, which leads to the emotional. Women are jump-started emotionally, which leads to the physical. If you can separate what he's watching from who you are (or aren't), you can reap the benefits of his arousal.

Women simply don't get it when it comes to hard-core porn. (Some women like soft-core, meaning *relationships* and—oh, yeah—a *plot* and clean feet.) When your spouse watches all that panting and tongue action, you think it's gross, stupid, and those boobs are *sooo* fake! Guys don't care that they're fake! And that's okay. Accept that you're not going to see eye to eye in this area, and recognize that it's unlikely he's going to leave you for some bimbette adult video star. At the same time, though, it may help you jump-start a flagging sex life. If you really are too offended to watch along with him, set up a VCR in another room for his viewing pleasure, then snuggle up with *your* version of "porn"—a steamy romance novel or a movie starring Tom Cruise, Val Kilmer, Cary Grant—and arrange a rendezvous after the final credits roll.

Adultery, too, is a way for men to feel like top dog again. To be in *control*. To get back in the chase. Men define infidelity much more loosely than women do. If a guy is more than twenty miles away from home (or two hundred miles for some purists), if his *wife* is out of town or cranky, if he doesn't love the girl or doesn't *say* he loves her, if she's a prostitute, if it's oral sex, he can justify sleeping around. Women, on the other hand, view lust in his *heart* as a betrayal.

Needless to say, there's history here. The male notion of adultery as no big deal is connected to the ancient notion of a wife as "property." Even the Bible backs this up. The Seventh Commandment, "Thou shalt not commit adultery," doesn't refer to adultery as we know it today. In the Old Testament, a married man commits adultery only if he has sex with another man's wife, or if he deflowers another man's fiancée. In the patriarchal society of ancient Israel, women were essentially considered a man's property, so having sex with another man's wife or betrothed was similar to stealing his ox—stealing something of value from the man.

On the other hand, sleeping with *unmarried* loose women ("loose" women being "unattached" and therefore considered sexually available to any man) wasn't a breach of God's law or man's rules. It wasn't adultery.

Jane, Tarzan, listen up here: Men most often cheat for sex; women cheat for affection. But understanding why your spouse strayed doesn't lessen the pain—at least not right away. When someone you trust betrays you, it feels awful. Go ahead and feel hurt. It may even feel like it's a little bit your fault, but *don't* go there. Blaming yourself for your spouse's indiscretions is like apologizing when your husband burps. He's gotta take responsibility for what he did. Assuming you love him and want to go on with the relationship, you are entitled to demand to know three things:

Number one, why it happened. "I was drunk" or "It just happened" or "I dunno" simply won't do. Both of you have to know how to be able to move on to the next step.

Number two, find out how both of you can be certain it will never happen again.

Number three, establish what's in it for you should he stray.

Without these three components, how can *either* of you trust him again? Make the compensation something *big* like a vacation to Italy or emerald earrings. If your spouse protests the deal, you'll know he (or she, as the case may be) isn't serious about being faithful. Your marriage may need a professional intervention to help you release the hurt, figure out what went wrong, and make it right again. Ask the three questions and sit quietly until you get an acceptable answer.

Once you have your answers, take all the time you need to lick your wounds. Infidelity *hurts*. Short-circuiting the pain will only make it last longer. If you decide that you want to repair your relationship, you've got to let go of blame. Blaming feels good only for a second; then it feels lousy because it pulls people apart instead of bringing them together. If you're still too angry to confront your spouse without pointing the finger, give it a little more time, separate for a while, or vent your rage elsewhere before sitting down to work things out.

JUNGLE GEMS

Understanding men and their sex lives means accepting these basic male notions about sex:

+ *Sex is primarily about an erection.*
+ *Penises are unpredictable.*
+ *Not being able to control a penis feels scary.*
+ *Scary feelings are unmanly; feeling unmanly makes your penis go down.*
+ *No erection, no sex.*
+ *Sex is safest when it's unthinking, unfeeling, just diving in and doing it.*

Boys to Men

THE SEX OF an embryo is determined in the sixth week of gestation, male hormones are produced at about eight weeks, and the hypothalamus sets puberty in motion at about age ten. Sexual differentiation and sexual orientation are genetic, but sexual *behavior* is taught. From the moment a little boy's dad tosses him in the air and calls him a "slugger" or tells him to "go out there and win!" he learns that aggression and dominance are good. From the moment he's told to stop touching himself "down there," he learns that masturbation is bad. From the moment he sees his little sister bat her baby blues and melt Daddy's heart, he understands that girls get what they want differently than boys do. Sexual roles and sexual stereotypes are enforced and reinforced throughout a child's life. Sexual images, and the messages they convey, are so pervasive and persuasive in our culture that no child is immune.

Some examples: The new G.I. Joe Extreme is so muscle-bound that his biceps are larger than his waist. He carries a machine gun. Barbie has a triple-D bust, size 2 butt, and feet in a permanent high-heel stance. Popeye finally married Olive Oyl after a *seventy-year* engagement. *Victoria's Secret* catalogs arrive monthly in the mail (to an estimated 80 percent *male* "readership"!), *Baywatch* babes run down the beach in slo-mo, *Pretty Woman* was a huge hit with the whole family, and professional wrestling is so popular, a former wrestler was elected governor of Minnesota.

The message: "Real" men are over-the-top aggressive, sexy women have huge, firm breasts and fit, tan bodies and are prancing about in lacy underwear forever ready for sex, guys never really *have* to marry their girlfriends, "nice" hookers (who look like Julia Roberts) get the rich guy (Alpha male, anyone?), and even if everybody knows it's fake, violence wins in the end.

Fathers teach their sons about sex; mothers teach their daughters. But most of the time, it's too little, too late—their kids have already "learned" about sex from their adolescent friends. These days, kids study "sex" education in school and end up learning more about AIDS than about love and lust or their own bodies and sensibilities.

Part of the problem with dads exclusively teaching sons about sex is the father's own unexpressed and unexamined ambivalent feelings. No dad does (or can) admit that he felt like a stud muffin before the kids were born. He was a lover, a date, a swashbuckling romantic hero. When his wife was pregnant, he wanted to shout, "Look what I did!" After the babies arrived, he felt less and less needed and often less wanted sexually. He felt as though his wife got what she wanted from him—she squeezed him dry—and now all she wants is a paycheck and a roof over their heads and help keeping everything clean or maybe even another baby or two. Talk about a real letdown. From *hot stuff* to *sperm donor* in one easy lesson. Plus, and this is really too scary to even admit, he doesn't quite feel the same way toward her sexually, either. She's a *mom.* She's no longer his sex slave, she's his child's *mommy.* It feels uncomfortable sometimes to have sex with her 'cause, really, the best sex is dirty sex. Animal, sweaty sex. And who can feel good about having dirty sex with a mom? It feels so . . . *wrong* in a bad way. Not to mention that to men, becoming a father means that they've become *their* fathers as well—a wanna-be Alpha (every dad is an Alpha to his son) who sees himself aging and constrained. If he admires his dad, he feels second best. If he deplores him, he feels even worse. He can't escape the family curse. Fatherhood is a mixed blessing. On the one hand, it's a sign of virility passing on the old DNA, *hubba, hubba,* ensuring immortality. On the other, it's feeling less relevant, less vital, and more estranged from the woman who used to make him feel all these things. Is it any wonder that men often stray during a wife's pregnancy (when she's most likely to feel especially betrayed) and that a pregnant father's greatest fear is that he's not the father of his unborn child? We've got to help men escape this prison.

That's the real (and real scary) stuff that dads don't say or even admit feeling. I'm certainly not suggesting that they *start* telling their kids about the animal sex they want to have with their mom. What I am suggesting is that mothers talk to their sons about sex and fathers talk to their *daughters*. Sex is demystified that way; plus, one-sided misconceptions, fears, and mixed feelings don't get handed down from parent to child. When moms talk to their sons and dads talk to their daughters, each side can see the other point of view. Moms have the chance to tell their boys how important it is for a woman to feel cherished; dads can tell their girls that sex is more of a physical than an emotional experience for many guys. Both parents can reverse some of the false sexual stereotypes their kids are bound to internalize as they grow up.

WILD THINGS

Q. *Full-grown male deer who've lost their antlers (a sign of status and virility) are destined to a life of:*
   a. Celibacy.
   b. Injury.
   c. Clandestine sex.

A. *Clandestine sex.* Size definitely matters in the stag herd, so a male deer who's lost his "size," his antlers, has to be creative. Since he knows he'll lose any fight over control of the harem with an antlered male, he doesn't try. Instead, he sneaks into the herd unnoticed and grabs a quickie before the dominant male catches him. It's not unlike the ninety-eight-pound weakling who doesn't bother with the studs at

Muscle Beach. Instead, he starts an Internet company and steals girls through his stock price.

Q. *The Jacobson's organ, crucial to a male lion's mating success, is located on:*
   a. The roof of his mouth.
   b. The tip of his penis.
   c. The pads beneath his paws.

A. *The roof of his mouth.* This scent organ can evaluate the aroma of female urine and determine whether she's in heat. Male lions on the prowl curl their lips back, tilt their heads up, and let the scent waft into their mouths. When his *mouth* tells him she's ready, he's ready. Talk about mouth-watering . . . !

Humans have a sensory sex signal as well, only we inhale through our noses. Without our even realizing it, certain natural body scents called pheromones attract and repel us. They say attraction is in the *eyes*, but it's probably first in the nose.

HIStory

A MAN IS NOT only the product of his sexual upbringing, but of sexual evolution as well, and the history of sexuality is primarily the history of men satisfying their desires, gaining status, and controlling women by keeping them barefoot and pregnant. And, for men, it's about ensuring that the offspring are indeed his. That's why territories were established and social hierarchies so fiercely defended. Alpha males don't want Omegas

swimming in their gene pool. It's also why the phallus is wor-
shiped in so many ancient religions and why phallic symbols
appear throughout ancient art and religious artifacts. The penis is
the symbol of fertility, and fertility is the basis of life. (Hey, I'm
not going to be the one to question the Washington Monument.)

Sexuality in early Athens was geared toward pleasing the
male citizens who held all the power in the state. Women, slaves,
foreigners, and boys were all made sexually available to men. Later,
in Rome, marriage and adultery laws were enacted as a sort of aris-
tocratic self-defense. Upper-class Italian men were fooling around
so much that no one was replenishing the clan with quality stock.
And marriages in the Middle Ages were arranged by men because,
as one scholar put it, "no sensible family would allow the posses-
sion of valuable property to be jeopardized by casual alliances."

The notion of women as sexual property continued as our own
country came into being. The Pilgrims were *Puritans* after all. And
once religion took hold of sexuality, shame took hold as well. (The
Catholic Church still doesn't allow birth control, other than the
highly unreliable rhythm method and incredibly unpopular absti-
nence method.) In Ireland as recently as the 1950s, unwed mothers
and "fallen women" were quietly whisked off to a life of slave labor in
convent laundries! The men who fathered their children or deflow-
ered them were left alone to marry and build lives on the "outside."

Perhaps the most significant event in sexual history, however, took place in 1916 when Margaret Sanger opened the first
birth-control clinic in the United States. Contraception shifted
sexual control into the hands of women. It allowed women to
explore sexuality without fear of pregnancy. Birth control altered a
gazillion years of evolution in a heartbeat or two. Once a woman no
longer had to be "barefoot and pregnant," she became an adult

with sexual options similar to those of her male counterpart. Indulging her or her partner's appetite no longer was a necessary monthly fertility lottery—she was no longer at the mercy of either.

Working It Out Together

BEING MALE in the millennium means having less and less to do evolutionarily. A guy's job used to be to impregnate the women and protect the tribe; women can now protect themselves, and they can *buy* first-rate sperm at a bank. This means males are feeling less valued and more out of control. Which means men need understanding and compassion while we take quantum leaps together. And women need to express what they *really* want. A friend of mine, who'd gained a few pounds over the holidays, confessed that her sex life was being crushed under her weight. Though she's not fat, she *felt* enormous . . . and ashamed. "I kept inventing ways to put off having sex with my husband," she told me. "I didn't want him to see me until I'd lost the weight." Finally her husband asked what on earth was going on. She just blurted out the truth, saying, "I feel fat. I'm afraid you're going to look at me and be so turned off you won't want me." Of course, he wanted her even more at that moment. First of all, he didn't care that she was a little chubby; secondly, he loved her; and thirdly, he felt close to her because she was brave enough to trust him with that information.

Shame separates us from one another. The whole point about any kind of intimacy is trusting somebody with who you really are. No one wants to be loved for their *potential*—who they might be or should be or could be. The only way to let someone love you for who you are at that moment is to admit who you really are—not only to someone else, but to yourself.

Look, sex is a vulnerable area for everybody. Men and women ultimately want the same things: closeness and intimacy. Both sides get scared, and everybody has a different speed, path, memory of what works and what doesn't work, and tolerance for the uncertainty involved in opening yourself up to another person. That's why sex is often a barometer for relationships. When a couple is in sync beneath the sheets, other areas of their relationship are usually in sync as well. When things aren't so hot in the bedroom, it's time to sit down in the living room and figure out what's really going on.

It's *never* too late to improve, revise, refine, refresh, and reinvent a sex life. Couples who've slept on either end of the bed for years can literally come together in the middle. When talking about sex, it's crucial to follow three basic communication rules: Don't argue in bed, start each sentence with "I feel" instead of "you are," and leave blame where it belongs—out of sight, out of mind. It's not payback time for women. It's time for accepting both males and females as sexual beings in need of love, attention, and empathy.

QUANTUM

MEN

Just as a woman can say no, you can say no, too.

Accept that you *aren't* always ready for sex—it's okay to admit it.

Be aware that your sex drive doesn't have to match hers; hers doesn't have to match yours.

Tell her how much you want her during the *day*.

Understand the difference between physical affection and sex. If the first *always* leads to the other, she's going to feel used.

WOMEN

Never take impotence personally.

Understand that every man is fearful that he'll be caught wanting at the critical moment.

Believe that pornography has nothing to do with you or his love for you; porn is his security blanket and insurance policy all rolled into one (so to speak).

Know that masturbation is his way of checking out the equipment to make sure everything is in working order.

Schedule sex on both your calendars. Spontaneity is great, but making a place for important stuff is the only way to ensure it'll get done!

LEAPS

Seven

Roaring

Men and Communication

MOUNTAIN GORILLAS of Central Africa grunt and grumble and hoot and occasionally screech at one another as the elders discipline the youngsters, indicate affection, and express pleasure at particularly delicious leaves. But when an intruder stumbles upon their enclave, a silverback's first reaction is absolute, rock-solid *silence.* The instant a male gorilla feels threatened, he clams up until he has assessed the danger. If the threat continues, he pulls out all the stops—crashing through the forest, pounding his chest with his fists, and hooting so fiercely he can be heard a mile away.

Vervet monkeys of the African grasslands bark to warn others of danger, dominant wolves snarl to keep lesser wolves at bay, deer stags of the Scottish Highlands roar to alert would-be competitors not to mess with their harems, and leopard toads from

West Africa vibrate their vocal cords to emit a loud, deep croak admonishing, "Don't even *think* of leaping onto my lily pad."

Male animals in the wild communicate for three major reasons: to assert dominance, defend territory, and warn the clan of danger. And, oh yeah, some male animals, like the American sage grouse, use songs of love to attract a mate—perhaps because the female sage grouse (older, wiser, and crankier—at least by description) won't make herself sexually available until she's been wooed.

The Human Animal

O NE OF THE major differences between humans and animals is the language of spoken words. One of the major similarities between men and animals is *communication*. Animals communicate, but they don't talk. Men also communicate, but they don't always use words to do it. (Okay, before you write me a gazillion letters, I realize that *parrots* "talk." But they use language to mimic more than communicate.) The notion that men are lousy at communication simply isn't true. Guys communicate very well with one another, coworkers, coaches, business associates, mortgage brokers. When the situation calls for a language in which they're well-versed, i.e., *business-speak*—you know, facts, numbers, spreadsheets, bottom lines—they converse very effectively.

Guys talking business is all about turf, dominance, and pounding chests, which is something lots of men like to do. Talking about *feelings* is another matter altogether. All that mushy, emotional, abstract, vulnerable stuff—*personalspeak*—makes most men squirm. Isn't there a ball game on? That's why women often accuse men of being uncommunicative. What they're really saying is guys don't communicate the way women want them to. In a word, they don't talk about *feelings* . . . or at least they don't say what women want them to say.

A woman asks a man, "Do you love me?" He answers, "I'm here, aren't I?" To a man, that's a perfectly legitimate response to a question about his feelings. In his mind, his love is proven every day he comes home from work, every evening he *stays* home, every night he beds his woman, and every Friday he hands over his paycheck. For men, actions really do speak louder than words.

Physical proximity equals caring; literally *keeping in touch* is communication. It's the way men have learned to communicate with one another—side by side in silence—and the expectation many men carry into a relationship with a woman. His physical presence by her side communicates his love and regard for her. For most women, walking the walk is nothing if you can't also talk the talk. Women want their men to *say,* "I love you," "I'm sorry," "I'll never leave you" and "Raphaelite women have the sexiest thighs," "Cindy Crawford is too skinny," and "That sexy new sales assistant won't age well."

Men have learned that noise can be dangerous and silence can be powerful. Noise identifies their position, lets "the enemy" know where they are. Since men have been trained to constantly compete with one another, strive to be top dog, struggle to stay there, and make it all look easy, letting other males know their whereabouts is instinctively unnerving.

Males live their lives by the wisdom of the great masculine forebears: Calvin Coolidge once said, "I have noticed that nothing I never said ever did me any harm." Teddy Roosevelt preached the gospel of speaking softly and carrying a big stick. Boil it all down and you have an entire gender operating under the assumption that their words can be misconstrued and used against them.

If you've ever wondered why some guys are loath to speak up at a meeting or "put it in writing," it's because words can make you look stupid as quickly as they can make you look smart. And guys will do almost anything to avoid looking stupid and inadequate. They can't grin sheepishly (or *sissyishly*) and say, "Whoops! There I go running off at the mouth again!" Since men are constantly competing with one another, silently scoring points against "the enemy" (who is anyone able to usurp their position in the pack), anything that might make them look foolish feels *dangerous*. And since men value sticking together, standing in the trenches, watching one another's backs, trusting one another with their very lives, a loose cannon is a liability. Loose lips sink ships. Macho men are strong, silent types, the Clint Eastwoods who command respect with three brief words: "Make my day."

Ever wonder why . . .

. . . men *whistle* at women to let them know they find them attractive? Whistling is a human mating call, not unlike the gecko's chirping sound that invites female geckos to come on over. But if you've ever passed a construction site, you've no doubt noticed that it's not a very *successful* way to get a date. What can I say? There's a major difference between attracting attention and attracting *positive* attention. Guys, think quantum leaps.

Men have also learned the "golden" rule: *Silence is golden.* Silence is a sign of power, intelligence, self-assurance, wisdom. Men who say nothing are thought to have lots on their mind; women who speak their mind are thought to be out of control, to be chatterboxes. Silence gives time to assess the danger. Silence in the face of a "threatening" situation ("Where were you last night?" or "We have to talk") allows men enough time to muster the troops, plot a counterattack, and decide which response is most effective: pulling out all the stops, pounding his chest, and hooting, or barking, snarling, roaring, croaking, or wooing and hoping for the best.

Silence in a relationship is a power tool for many men. Some guys might even consider silence as "crafty" (gotcha—that's the definition of passive/aggressive). It's using silence to make someone come to *you* and do the talking or acting. It's manipulation with the emphasis on the *man.* Guys understand that women *want* them to talk (well, at least they *say* they do). Women ask, beg, cajole, trick, bribe—anything to get their men to open up. Withholding something that someone wants puts you in the driver's seat. It puts you in control of the relationship. Once you *share,* they've got it, too! *Not* sharing means hanging on to the prize, which is the power position.

A caller, thirty-six, recently told me she was going nuts because her husband had been picked as a juror on a criminal case that was expected to last for two months. She confessed to being sort of a crime junkie and was dying to hear all about it from an insider's point of view. "But he won't say a word!" she moaned. "The judge told him not to talk about the case, and he's taken a vow of absolute silence." The worst part of it, she explained, was that she was used to sharing *everything* with him. She was sure she could crack his resolve by swearing not to talk about the case, by begging, by insisting that the judge didn't mean he couldn't talk about the case with his *wife*. But he wouldn't budge.

In a world of actions speaking louder than words, it may be considered admirable that our juror wouldn't violate his oath. It was also a very powerful position for him to be in. He was saying to his wife, "What I'm doing is important, *I'm* important for doing it, and I'm going to continue feeling important by being strong, not giving in, and maintaining my silence." He was saying, "I have something you want, but I'm too important to give it to you." The more she pursued him, the stronger he felt and the further he pulled away from her. She was feeling left out, inferior, powerless, and hurt that he didn't consider her an extension of him (which is likely how she views herself).

What this woman was describing is a classic distancer/pursuer dynamic in many relationships. Typically, the female pursues and the male distances. The more she goes after him to communicate with her, the more he clams up. The more he clams up, the more desperately she tries to pry him open. The cycle continues until, eventually, you have an angry woman and a withdrawn man and both sides are complaining that *he/she doesn't get it.*

Men also opt for silence for *physical* reasons. A study done in 1988 by two psychologists, John Gottman and Robert Levenson, found that confrontations, or the anticipation of confrontations, activate a much more intense, unpleasant physiological response in men than women. Their heart rate increases, as does their galvanic skin response; they get headaches, tightness in the chest, a queasy stomach—a sort of head-to-toe emotional twister. It feels so lousy that most men do whatever they can to avoid it—withdraw, slam out of the room, tune out, holler (to feel back in control), lash out (to feel physically back in charge), say little, or say nothing at all. Jane, what's going on here is a behavior that many men learn as boys: Don't confront and communicate your feelings; your anger is dangerous and unacceptable, so go to your room!

Ever wonder why . . .

. . . guys get *angry* when women try to force them to talk? Since the subtleties of language likely evolved as a primarily female tool mothers used to communicate with their children, some men feel that talking reduces them to the status of "boy." Real *men* stand side by side in silence. They hunt, stalk prey, mate, read *The Wall Street Journal*—none of which requires any talking at all. Women tend to be the teachers and reinforcers of language; they sit face-to-face and talk to their babies. So when men are prodded by their women to open up, it feels like Mommy insisting that they eat their string beans. Men don't like to feel bossed, especially by a woman, and often get angry when it feels as if they are.

Many men are reluctant to talk as much as women do because they also feel prattle is really *boring*. A guy listening to his wife recount every detail of carpooling, kids' squabbles, mother-in-law grievances, and complaints of day-to-day relationships are reluctant to put others in the same position. They want to talk about active, exciting stuff—conflict resolution, the triumph of good over evil—in a word, sports or the stock market. Both men and women may talk "facts," but if men view the facts as trivial or uninteresting to them, the woman is accused of prattling.

Plus, on some level guys realize that their women very likely *don't* want to hear what's on their minds, if it's not her, relevant to her, or interesting to her. Not just sexually, either. Don't believe me? Watch a woman's eyes glaze over as her husband details the spreadsheets of the latest merger, or her boyfriend lists baseball statistics or sacks per game in the NFL. Men don't want to be rejected by their women, and they certainly don't want to be considered *dull.* Women tend to force the issue more—they'll insist that their man listen even if he doesn't want to.

Women want to be heard, but men understand that women would be horrified, petrified, bored, hurt, insulted if they told them what was *really* on their minds. She'd freak out and he'd have to waste a lot of energy calming her down, or she'd pout and sulk and he'd never get any sex. Which is what *he* wants at all cost. So he clams up.

Women make the mistake of assuming that men are withholding their innermost feelings of *love.* They assume, because they think about their man often during the day, that he is often thinking about them like he said he was during their courtship. (Understand that thinking about *sex* with someone and thinking about someone aren't the same thing.) Most women feel certain that once they break through his tough outer shell, a loving, caring, emotionally available male will emerge who is like her in every way but between the legs. And that's exactly what scares the daylights out of guys. Talking feels like being a girl. Being a girl is unmanly. Feeling unmanly feels like the worst feeling in the world.

Jane, when it comes to getting your guy to *talk* already, understand that you probably don't want information as much as you want closeness. Being face-to-face with him makes you feel as safe as it makes him feel threatened. Neither is good and neither is bad; it's simply learned behavior that's been in place for years. Try translating *his* vocabulary for intimacy. Does he reach for your hand while he watches a football game, does he wear the sweater you knitted for him, does he bring you flowers after you two have an argument? Asking him to communicate the way *you* want him to (with words) may be asking a lot initially. It may make him feel like he did when his mom asked him to clean his room. It just makes him dig in his heels and say, "She can't control me!" Besides, it doesn't work.

What *does* work when you want someone to talk more is for you to listen more. It's as simple as that. It may take a little time, and may make you feel sort of queasy when he says stuff you don't want to hear. But take a deep breath, keep your mouth shut, don't rush to "fix" his situation, look for his *non*verbal expressions of love, and let him relearn that talking isn't for wimps, it's for real men in real grown-up relationships.

Tarzan—ironically, if you want your woman to talk *less*, listening to her more will do the trick. Volunteer to talk yourself without waiting till she's crying tears of frustration. Talking is her way of building a bridge of intimacy between the two of you. She sees you tune out and tries even harder to reach you. How? Through the one way she learned how to bond with others: conversation. When she's talking to you, she has your attention— which is what she really wants anyway. (As long as we're talking about silence or not—women who are truly secure in a relationship are secure enough to trust silence—he'll talk more if you talk less.)

Finally, most men are aggressive at work and passive at home. Which is why so many women feel they're married to the ultimate passive-aggressive. Being passive-aggressive means having a hidden agenda, manipulating another person by using guilt, shame, blame—whatever it takes to get what you want. Instead of *admitting* what you want, claiming your own emotions, you try and punch somebody's buttons to get what you want without admitting you actually want it. That way, there's no debt incurred. It's "Hey, it was *your* idea, not mine." A passive-aggressive husband sighs and says, "Don't worry about me—we'll be okay. The kids and I will eat leftovers and it probably won't even damage their psyches. Besides, we can all go over to my mom's house next week for a real home-cooked meal." A more honest way of phrasing it would be "My mom cooked for me and I wish you'd do the same."

When what he really wants is stated directly, both husband and wife can deal with it, negotiate a cooking schedule, or talk about the fact that Mom didn't bring home half the bacon. When someone is being passive-aggressive, the message is delivered, but it's coded, sullen, insulting, and when the recipient feels angry, manipulated, and controlled, the passive-aggressive person can then plead complete ignorance—"Hey, I *said* we'd eat leftovers!"—while implying something quite different. It's a nasty way to do business; everybody loses in the long run. Asking for what we want doesn't guarantee we'll get it, but it goes a long way toward improving the probability and encouraging a loving relationship of equal, responsible, straightforward, honest partners. Jane, don't be tempted to interpret for your man—you're not his mom. He's a grown-up, sentient being. If you listen, he'll talk—perhaps slowly, haltingly, and less than glibly—but be patient and *silent*.

JUNGLE GEMS

*Understanding men and communication means
accepting these basic male notions:*

✦ *Men prefer to be side-by-side rather than face-to-face.*

✦ *Actions speak louder than words.*

✦ *"We need to talk" are the four most feared words in a
relationship.*

✦ *Talking feels like entrapment.*

✦ *When trapped, men will do anything—withdraw,
lash out, fall into a coma—to break free.*

Boys to Men

BOYS LEARN EARLY on that *talking* isn't the best way to get
what they want. Human animals, like all animals, learn how
to adapt to their environment to survive. A friend of mine
has a dog whose breakfast time is seven-thirty A.M., but he'd get
hungry earlier and wake my friend up by whining at seven o'clock.
Annoyed, she'd say a strong "No!" and fall back asleep. After a few
days, her dog understood that whining wasn't going to get him any
kibble, so instead, he sidled up to her ear and *whisper*-whined at
seven A.M. Under his breath, he "whined" softly in her ear to let
her know he was ready for some chow. Laughing because she
thought his behavior was so cute, she got up and fed him at seven.
Mission accomplished. For *Fido*. He adapted his behavior to survive . . . and it worked. Which is just what kids do. They figure out

how to "whisper-whine" or do whatever it takes to get Mom and Dad to give them what they want.

As a kid who was always pushing the envelope, I learned that the best way to get out of a spanking, lecture, or grounding was to make my parent (usually *Dad*) laugh. In that moment, I had leveled the playing field, deflected the anger, and dissipated the anger and intensity. I was communicating his dominance without seeming subservient or fearful. Or maybe I was just being the court jester to the king.

Since a child's very existence relies on the benevolence of Mom and Dad, young children live and die to please their parents. Kids learn that survival depends upon learning what Mom and Dad expect of them and giving them what they want. That, in turn, gives kids what they want—love, attention, and affection from the *source* of their life and survival.

Even the most well-intentioned parents teach boys how to communicate like "boys" and girls how to communicate like "girls." The first time a parent says to a little boy, "Go outside and ride your bike," and says to a little girl, "Go in your room and play with your dolls," he or she communicates what is expected of that child. The message is "Good little boys are active; good little girls are passive." Sports don't require much talking; playing with dolls is *all* talking. When Susie falls down and Mom says, "Tell me where it hurts," and when Johnny falls down and Dad says, "Big boys don't cry," both kids learn how to communicate.

When Dad freaks out because his son plays with dolls or follows Mom around expressing his love for her, boys learn that "guys" don't do that. When Mom freaks out because her son says he was in his room masturbating, and she gives him a hug and a cookie when he says he was in his room reading a good book, boys learn that lying pays off. And when kids see Dad giving Mom the silent treatment, or Mom chatting at the dinner table while Dad stares off into space, they learn how men and women act with one another.

Boys learn that "talking" is for girls and "action" is for boys. *Aggressive* talking—hollering, bullying, teasing, taunting—feels more acceptable. It's about dominance, and that feels more comfortable than vulnerability. Boys also learn that "standing up for themselves" in the face of a real or perceived threat (bigger kid, bossy girl) is the manly thing to do. It's the human equivalent of crashing through the forest, pounding your chest. But talking honestly about fear, pain, need, love, and sex is a big no-no unless you want to be considered a sissy or a pervert. Either one guarantees rejection, and who volunteers to be rejected? So, from earliest childhood, boys learn to communicate in *nonverbal* ways. They learn to create intimacy with *proximity* instead of chitchat. They learn to be side-by-side instead of face-to-face. To *do* instead of *say*. Girls learn the exact opposite—which causes all kinds of problems later when her "pillow talk" is a sweet nothing and his is a snore.

Look, part of language is a *physiological* function of a portion of the brain's cortex called Broca's area. This section of the brain, located above the left ear, tells the mouth, throat, tongue, and vocal cords to produce speech. The motor cortex triggers the impulses that produce sounds, other regions of the motor cortex coordinate the sounds, and Wernicke's area of the temporal lobe helps us understand what's being said. Babies usually speak their first word at about twelve months; by age two, their vocabulary has expanded from "mama" and "dada" to about 270 words. By age six, it's ten times that many. Human animals have innate characteristics that enable them to learn language, but *communication* skills must be *taught*. Complex communication is the essence of human connection. Without it, we might as well be, well, *animals*.

Ever wonder why . . .

. . . guys get all squirmy when women say, "We need to talk"? It's the emotional equivalent of hollering, "Throw-up!" on a crowded subway—increased heart rate, queasy palms, and a mad dash for the nearest exit. In childhood, kids use words as tendrils to wrap around Mom and Dad to make sure they pay attention. They ask endless questions as a way to keep Mommy and Daddy close. Why is the sky blue? How does an airplane fly? What happened to the dinosaurs? Most weary parents learn to *ignore* the constant barrage. Saying to a guy, "We need to talk," makes him feel as if a tendril's reaching out to ensnare him. He feels trapped in the position of parent—about to get an endless barrage that he's not going to be able to ignore.

Jane, Tarzan—if you want to raise children who communicate well (who doesn't?), it's crucial to first accept that kids need lots and lots of love and attention. Sometimes it seems as if they need attention around the clock, which can feel overwhelming, but every parent is responsible for understanding, not necessarily meeting, their child's needs. That's what parenting is all about. Good parents help their children get *specific*. Kids don't always know exactly what they want. They just feel icky or lonely or excited, and they want Mommy and Daddy nearby. Learning how to identify precisely what you want, and ask for it, is the basis of excellent communication. Parents who can teach their children these skills will raise kids who can communicate very effectively.

First, discourage whining. Whining is how kids say, "Pay attention to me! And if you don't, I'm going to make it so uncomfortable for you, you'll eventually give in." Whiny kids grow into whiny adults, and people like to hang around *winners*, not whiners. The best way to stop kids from whining is to say, "Tell me what you want." This simple sentence empowers kids, gives them a way to sort out their jumbled feelings, and helps them get specific. If they can't come up with an immediate, specific answer, tell them to take five minutes to think about it, then come back to you with an answer when they're ready.

Secondly, train yourself not to instantly react negatively when your child tells you something you don't want to hear. I know it's hard to keep calm when your kid says, "Yeah, Mom, I've tried drugs" or "No, I'm not a virgin anymore," but simply say, "I'm glad you told me the truth. I need a few minutes to digest what you said." You don't always need to have the right answer right away. But the *wrong* answer is punishing your child for telling the truth. I'm not suggesting kids get away with whatever they want. Instead, you can learn how to praise the truth-telling and punish the act. Otherwise, you only train kids to tell the truth when it's *easy*.

Communication is really hard stuff because to communicate effectively, you first have to know how you feel. Then you have to be able to conceptualize it, verbalize it in a way somebody else can understand, and stick around so they can go through the process in reverse. The person with whom you're trying to communicate has to figure out what his or her reaction is, conceptualize it—go from a sense to a feeling to a description—and be able to respond in a way *you* can understand. Even if both people are very intuitive and articulate, if they're speaking two different languages, both sides are sunk. It's important, too, not to make the other person defensive. If he or she shuts down, nobody's going to be able to communicate anything.

WILD THINGS

Q. *The male red-winged blackbird communicates his territorial dominance by:*
   a. Chirping louder than any other bird.
   b. Varying his bird calls throughout his territory.
   c. Holding a note longer than any other bird.

A. *Varying his bird calls throughout his territory.* The male blackbird tries to fool would-be invaders into thinking his territory is occupied by *several* birds. He flies to different points in his domain, singing out a variety of bird songs. This enables him to command a larger space and attract more females since size also matters in the bird world— males with the biggest *territories* get the girl. (Hey—biggest seems to count *everywhere!*) In the male animal, as well as male *human* animal, world, there's safety and solidarity in numbers . . . even if those "numbers" are only perceived.

Q. *The loudest noise in the animal kingdom is created by the:*
   a. Howler monkey.
   b. Asian elephant.
   c. Blue whale.

A. *Blue whale.* The deep-toned call of the one-hundred-foot blue whale vibrates through the ocean for half a minute at 180 decibels—a volume so loud it would deafen human ears. Though no one is sure exactly why whales wail, it's most likely to contact family members or let other whales know they are ready to mate. Deep-sea communication among animals is literally uncharted water. Scientists believe they may communicate a wide variety of ideas and feelings. However, as with some human communications, it's all in the interpretation. The listener may be "hearing" what he or she *wants* to hear.

Q. *The male gibbon "sings" to his mate in a nearby tree to:*
   a. Strengthen their bond as a couple.
   b. Warn other gibbons to stay out of their "home."
   c. Indicate by their back-and-forth duet how high up they both are in the social hierarchy.

A. *All of the above.* Gibbons mate for life. Their treetop communiqués with each other are a sort of shorthand that they've developed over time, just like long-married human couples do. It's a way for them to understand each other, keep in touch, and let other gibbons know that there's no messing around with their love *thang*. (Hmmm . . . I wonder if they begin to look alike, and look like their pets as well?)

HIStory

N O ONE IS SURE exactly when our ancestors first identified specific objects with specific words, but man has been communicating since the beginning of time. Skull fossils of *Homo habilis*, or the prehistoric "Handy Man," show that early humans had the cranial capacity for speech. But any type of noise could be deadly to men on the hunt, so it's likely that while men practiced stillness and silence, women practiced a primitive language with one another and their children.

Women used language to instruct, entertain, and bond; men used language to warn one another of impending danger or scare off would-be predators. Historically, men only had to communicate a limited number of things: warning, satisfaction, anger. But if you're dealing with small children, you need to communicate a whole bunch of variations on those same themes. Warnings could be "Don't bother me now" or "Get back here right now, it's really dangerous!" Nuance and consistency became crucial (otherwise, you were always crying wolf). Plus women had to communicate with one another because they were taking care of one another's babies. Obviously, if you're communicating over distance, communication has to be very loud, straightforward, and simple. Once you're dealing with small creatures and one another and you're nearby, language develops subtle variations.

The earliest forms of *written* communication—cave drawings—show bears and rhinos and mammoths presumably in an attempt to warn and inform other proto-humans about the perils in the world. Other early nonverbal forms of communicating, performed primarily by men, include beating drums, smoke signals, and light beacons. Men needed to communicate with other men, other warriors or hunters, far away, while women had their children, and the other women in the tribe, literally *close at hand.*

For those women, speaking face-to-face was the most effective way to communicate. They never needed to shout—they were within earshot. Men, on the other hand, needed to develop more and more nonverbal ways to communicate as the world grew larger and they were responsible for marking, guarding, defending, tending, hunting in, and protecting bigger and bigger territories. They needed to communicate with lookouts and scouts; they needed to know where the enemy was without the enemy identifying his position. They needed to "speak" to one another without saying a word.

Fast-forward a bunch of centuries, and you can see that the history of labor also contributed to gender differences in communication. Men were alone working the fields; women and children were together working the kitchen. Soldiers were silent on the battlefield; women were grouped together making bandages and keeping the homes fires burning. Male factory work coupled men with *machines;* working women became teachers, nurses, and nannies. Even today, most teachers, nurses, and nannies are women, while priests, spies, security guards, soldiers, chess players, truck drivers, and golfers—professions that require silence and solitude—are generally men. If, historically, male survival depended upon verbal interaction, women would never be able to shut men up.

Working It Out Together

I F SILENCE AND solitude have traditionally been a male means of survival, modern men have now learned that silence and solitude in a relationship don't cut it anymore. Fifty years ago, women may not have *liked* it that their men were uncommunicative, but most were financially and socially dependent on their husbands or fathers, so what could they say? Open up or I'm outta here? Hey, women had to survive, too, so most accepted the status quo.

Now women aren't as dependent on men, so they can speak their minds. And men realize that to get what they want from women (sex, stability, children, companionship, clean socks), they'd better give women what they want, too. And what women want is *communication*.

The challenge before both men and women is one of *definition*. Women define communication as "reassurance" and sharing what's on their minds. Women want to hear that they are loved twenty-four hours a day. Men define communication as "problem-solving." Men want women to *ooh* and *aah* as they talk about being Masters of the Universe. The solution for both sides is to meet each other halfway. Women: Say to your man, "If at some point you're ready to leave me, please tell me." He'll say, "Oh, okay," and you have to sit tight and sit *quiet* and trust him. If you don't trust your man, leave him. Men: Say to your woman, "I need you to listen to me right now." She'll say, "Oh, okay," and you have to risk telling her the scary stuff as well as the studly stuff. Couples who build a life together, instead of two lives that *live* together, will have built-in topics of conversation that interest both partners. Talking about the kids and the office is great, but exploring the whole world together will bring you closer to each other—conversationally as well as emotionally. The best way to encourage someone to talk is to practice listening. Women have a responsibility to *really* listen when their men talk. (I hear far more men complain that women never listen than women complain that men never talk. Women gripe that men never tell them what they want to *hear*.) Men have a responsibility to participate in the emotional care and feeding of the relationship. If a guy feels himself shutting down, and shutting his partner *out*, he needs to take a deep breath and bring himself back to the present moment. Anyone who's not used to opening up can feel threatened and frightened when they do. Dealing with *right now* helps the moment feel less overwhelming.

By anybody's definition, communication means *connection*. It comes from the same roots as the words *communal*, *communion*, *community*, and *common*, as in "all the things we have in *common*." Communication brings people together in the same way *excommunication* separates.

A woman, engaged to be married in five months, called my radio program telling me about her recurring dream. "I keep dreaming that my fiancé doesn't want to go through with the wedding and I freak out," she said. I asked her how he feels in real life, and she said she mentioned the dreams to him and he told her he's totally in favor of marrying her. Bingo. By telling her fiancé about her anxiety dreams, she put him in the position of knowing that she'd freak out if he backed out of the wedding or mentioned even the tiniest misgiving. His reassurance to her might have been the truth, but he also might have been telling her what he knew she wanted to hear. Offering that reassurance is something most men are trained early on to do. When you tell the truth ("Yeah, Mom, I was masturbating in my bedroom"), women freak out.

Instead of dumping her dream on him, she might have gar-
nered a more authentic response by saying, "I want to make sure
this is the right move for both of us. If you have second thoughts,
please tell me. I'll be hurt, but I'll survive. I'd rather know the
truth." Then she has to do something that's very hard for most
women to do: be quiet and risk rejection. Let him make up—and
communicate—his own mind.

QUANTUM

MEN	WOMEN
Pick a male friend you feel you can dominate and admit a weakness.	Don't view engaging a man in a *debate* as "fun." It doesn't matter if he fights you or slinks away. Everybody gets bloodied and bruised and loses—even the "winner."
Practice sharing intimacies that aren't competitive.	
Take a course or play a sport in which you're not very good so you don't *have* to get a better grade or win.	Practice getting through to people, not *winning* an argument.
Keep a journal. This isn't a "Captain Kirk, Stardate 2133, we're searching out new life-forms" log. This is "feelings." (Don't worry, you don't have to show it to anyone.)	Fight the tendency to cry in the midst of a disagreement—men view it as manipulative and childish. Pause to regain your bearings. (Think Ninja warrior.)
Compliment somebody specifically.	Think through your points before you start talking.
Accept a compliment from somebody by just saying "thank you" without then giving a payback compliment.	Be very *specific*—figure out what you want and ask for it.
	Be quiet. (Silence can also be companionable.)

LEAPS

Eight

Plumage

Men and Appearance

MALE RAGGIANAS (or for those among us who aren't zool-ogists, birds of paradise) fan out their sweeping bright-orange plumes to dazzle any female who happens by. If no bodacious female birds—or is that redundant?—are around, that's okay. They display their fine feathers to other males—a sort of "I'll show you mine if you show me yours" so they can compare length and color and scope out the competition.

Male argus pheasants do the same. They look like chickens until aroused. That's when they unfold a glorious display of feath-ers, not unlike a peacock's, to dazzle their plain-Jane objects of desire. Lions have their manes, moose have their antlers, ele-phants have their tusks. Male animals in the wild have body mark-ings that indicate status, age, and sexual fitness. Their "plumage" is its own language, communicating how and where they belong in animal society.

In the animal kingdom, females pale in comparison to their male counterparts in the looks department (otherwise, I suppose we'd call it the animal *queen*dom). Even if moms weren't too busy carrying, having, feeding, and raising the youngsters to worry about showing off their plumage, all the guys would be drooling after them anyway. Why bother? Female animals need the human equivalent of short wash-and-wear hair, comfy sweatpants, and a housecoat that snaps up the front for easy breast-feeding. Their true colors are revealed through the hard work of childbirth and child care, not the showmanship of courting and competing.

HIStory

ISTORICALLY, HUMAN male plumage is about protection and position. Clothing itself evolved as a protection against climate—from animal skins in colder weather to loincloths when the heat was on. (Not to mention what a loincloth was intended to *protect*. Even from the earliest manifestation of male clothing, it was about the penis.)

Hair, too, is evolutionary evidence of nature's attempt to protect the body. When the world was physically dangerous at every turn, man was covered in a puffy cushion called *hair*. As danger became more mental and sexual—guys could steal your job, your woman—the arms, legs, and (one would hope) back lost much of its natural barrier against assault. What remained in full force was hair on the head, around the groin, and covering the heart on the chest. Body hair has evolved to the point of being man's natural means of protecting his vital organs: brain, penis, and heart. No wonder guys get upset when they lose their hair!

Look, mammals are the only animals that have real hair, and *all* mammals have hair. Even mammals that don't seem as if they have hair—like a rhinoceros or a whale—have hair somewhere on their adult body or had hair as embryos. So hair, in and of itself, is one thing that distinguishes us as warm-blooded vertebrates. In addition to language, an opposable thumb, and the ability to contemplate our own death while walking upright, hair is one of the characteristics that makes us human.

Hair is also one of the most visible and reliable identifiers of heredity. Different races have different inherited follicles, which produce distinctive types of hair. Asian and Native American hair grows from a straight follicle and is almost always coarse, straight, and black; African and Melanesian hair grows from a curved follicle, which produces spiraled, twisted strands; European hair grows from a straight follicle with an oval cross section, which produces both wavy and straight hair. Hair can even be a way to ensure parentage, because curly hair is a dominant trait.

Historically, groups of people have been identified by their hair and literally *classified* by it. People who didn't have hair like that of those in power were deemed second-class citizens and shunned from the *pack.* Which may explain why, today, some men wear hats even when it's warm outside, or baseball caps indoors or backward. Perhaps they are covering the most apparent evidence of their ancestry, the fact that they have little hair at all, or they're making an instantly visible statement of individuality or rebellion.

Copious amounts of hair have always been a symbol of courage and virility. Ancient Egyptian wall paintings depict long-haired warriors on the hunt. Samson's hair was the secret to his strength. Statues of Greek Olympic athletes show buffed-up *bearded* guys. Alexander the Great had a great head of hair. Japanese samurai had tons of thick, black hair, as did Geronimo and

Crazy Horse. And, hey, don't forget the modern romance version of the sexy squire, Fabio. Though hairstyles and lengths change, one thing remains the same: Hair is considered sexy. (Yeah, I know Sean Connery was voted *People* magazine's Sexiest Man Alive in 1989, but when he was playing "Bond, James Bond," his pate was covered, *toupee*-covered! Plus, the *rest* of the guys on *People* magazine's sexy list barely even *recede*. I mean, could JFK Jr., Tom Cruise, James Brolin, or Brad Pitt have any *more* hair on his head?!) Guys without a lot on top often feel the need to boost their sexual attractiveness in other ways . . . namely a big, fat, hairy *wallet.*

The highest heels, hugest pompadour, gaudiest crown, heaviest armor, fastest horse, most expensive watch, loudest tie—that "fat wallet" has taken many forms over the centuries. When it comes to men and their *clothes,* one of the earliest forms of male clothing to combine both protection and position was body *armor.* In the 1500s when Europeans seemed to be fighting with everybody, a complete suit of battle-ready body armor weighed about sixty-five pounds. And the metal to build a suit of armor was expensive. Only the wealthiest, strongest warriors could handle the cash and "carry" needed for a respectable ensemble. So wearing head-to-toe armor was a sign of high rank, wealth, or favor. And the higher the status, the more ornate the armor. Royalty created private armories to produce ornately etched, gilded breastplates and full suits. The most elaborate of these suits were given as gifts to other monarchs or worn in public processions as a sign of power and wealth.

Fashion itself has traditionally been the domain of the aristocracy. Before the industrial revolution, clothing was so costly to make and care for that only the rich could afford to wear the good stuff. And until the 1700s, men tended to dress even more flamboyantly than women, at least "decent" women. The guys wore high-heeled shoes, lacy collars, and powdered wigs. (Just look at paintings of America's forefathers to see some mighty fancy duds on dandified dudes. In the early days of portraiture, men looked like English aristocracy.)

Ever wonder why . . .

. . . so many guys dress like girls on Halloween? Think about it: A man is allowed to express his individuality in such a limited way—pants, shirt, jacket, tie. Women regularly and fashionably cross-dress. They are permitted to routinely wear fedoras, pantsuits, ties, men's shirts, clunky shoes—and it's considered stylish. A man veers away from the accepted mode of dress—say, he wears a pink shirt under his suit or an earring or a kilt—and *yikes!* He's labeled "gay" or perceived to be a loose cannon, not a team player, an upstart, a risk. He's not a member of the pack. It's why cross-dressing is so threatening for men. It's why guys dress in drag on Halloween when it's "safe" to do so. (Also understand that women dress as *hookers* on the same holiday. It doesn't take a psychologist to ask, "Can you say *repressed?*")

Clothing was a way to make an instant status statement without saying a word. It wasn't until democracy took hold and being the "common man" became the guy to be that American male fashion became less about separating the Alphas from the pack, and more about men as equals. By Abraham Lincoln's time, clothing was the embodiment of homespun humility. All of a sudden, plain waistcoats and yarn stockings became a way to fit in, not to mention a way to appear humble before God. Armani suits and power ties are a modern compromise between Puritanical forebears arm-wrestling with the spirit of Louis Quatorze and Henry the Eighth. What can I say? Guys will be guys and Alphas will rise up with competition—seeping into the boardroom, the bedroom, and, yeah, even the closet.

A man's clothing is a *marker.* It's an indication of his place in the pack. I can remember when I was growing up and my family had some lean years, my dad still bought his dress shirts at Brooks Brothers. For him it was important to show the outside world, and perhaps even the mirror, that he was "manly," still an Alpha male, meaning (to him) conservatively well-dressed in the best clothes.

Men are understandably and predictably able to identify the "secret" code of their clothing, the subtle distinction that may not be as evident to an outsider (read: *woman*). It's why Bill Gates can wear chinos to work, RuPaul can wear sequins, Ross Perot can have bad-hair days, Mick Jagger can wear eyeliner, and guys still respect their success. If you're powerful enough, you can break the rules. For most men, their clothing and hair, their *plumage,* needn't follow tradition as long as they can be "manly" in other ways—by getting the paycheck or the girl or (because one usually follows the other) *both.*

JUNGLE GEMS

*Understanding men and their plumage means accepting
these basic male notions:*

✦ *Adult male plumage is about compensating for
receding sexuality and men competing with one
another.*

✦ *Men believe that sexual potency begins to recede at
eighteen.*

✦ *Appearance is communication.*

✦ *Men communicate status to one another via their
appearance.*

✦ *Status equals sexual potency; the strongest sperm
survives.*

✦ *Sexual potency is communicated via appearance.*

The Human Animal

PREOCCUPATION WITH appearance is a major distinction between the human animal and the rest of the natural world, even though the reasons for our adornment are the same. Human *females* adorn themselves to attract a mate and stomp out the competition with five-inch stiletto heels. They spend thousands of dollars a year to reverse—or at least camouflage—nature by waxing, plucking, dyeing, dieting, perming, straightening, manicuring, pedicuring, liposucking, lifting, enhancing, resurfacing, and desperately trying to maintain a size six. Not to mention the endless search for the *perfect* red lipstick.

With guys, their appearance is about two things: penis and hair. Men seemingly care not one whit about noses, ears, butts, a beer gut, little spindly legs, a broken nose, or acne. If they have a full head of hair and a functioning penis, they're in business. They feel like *manly* men; the world can see it on top of their heads or in their Levi's, their woman can see it beneath the sheets—until they begin aging.

For most men, losing hair and virility means losing *it*. The signs of aging that matter to them—thinning on top and drooping down below—are signs that they are losing their top spot in the pack. They are vulnerable, no longer needed, no longer feared and revered. It's why men spend gobs of money on hair plugs, weaves, transplants, pieces, and Viagra (ten dollars a pill!). And when those stop helping enough, these men flash their *salaries* as plumage to get the girl and keep younger, stronger wolves at bay.

Tarzan, if you're losing your hair, listen up: Feeling upset, depressed, or even panicked about a receding hairline is under-standable. But the most common form of male hair loss, male pat-tern baldness (the receding hairline that eventually becomes a bald crown), is shared by 35 million guys. It's genetic and hor-monal, and if you're going to blame someone, holler at your mom, not your dad. Baldness is determined by a sex-linked autosomal recessive gene on the X chromosome. Check out your mama's brothers for a preview of things to come—you've got a fifty-fifty chance of ending up like they are. Sometimes topical treatments, like Minoxidil, or internal medications, like Propecia, can help slow the loss and even encourage regrowth, but results are seldom awesome. Transplants, hair weaves, and hairpieces can be expen-sive and obvious. A more fiscally efficient way to cope with hair loss is to deal with your underlying *feelings* about losing your hair.

What does having hair mean to you? Does it mean you're sexy? Virile? Attractive to the opposite sex? Warm in cold weather? Get specific. Ask yourself what being a "man" means to you. How do you feel about aging? What do you think women are most attracted to? What are your best characteristics? Write it all down in black and white. Be honest. If you think no woman will ever want to have sex with you if you're bald, admit it to yourself. Write "Having hair means . . . ," then fill in the blank. In a separate column, write "Being bald means . . . ," then fill in that blank.

Now look at those two statements. If you're like most men, both statements will be broad (excuse the pun) and general. That's okay. They'll probably look something like "Having hair means I'm sexy. Being bald means I'm a loser." Whatever you write down, as long as it's real for you, is *right*. What I want you to consider, however, is the difference between a *feeling* and a *reality*. While it may *feel* like being bald is being a loser, is it *real*? (Hey, bald— even shaved—is totally *in* for at least the moment.) Are all bald guys losers? Think Telly Savalas, Michael Jordan, Carl Reiner, and our buddy Sean Connery, who feels so secure he'll even show up in a kilt.

Once you figure out how you really feel, deep down, about losing your hair, you can also figure out how real your feelings really are. I'm not suggesting that they don't *feel* incredibly real and powerful, but I am suggesting that reality can be very powerful, too. Once we let our feelings define us, we run the risk of getting lost in a maze of emotions. Feeling what's there is good; not looking at what's real isn't so hot.

And Jane, if your Tarzan if getting a bit thin up on top, understand that hair loss to men is the equivalent of weight gain to women: It makes men feel unsexy, undesirable, and unmanly.

Telling him, "It's okay that you're losing your hair," will probably make him feel like a little boy, too. His mommy is patting him on the head and saying, "It's okay that you wet the bed." He's not going to believe you. Most guys don't want to "hear" that it's okay to go bald, they want to "feel" it. If you really are okay with your man's hair loss, why mention it at all? You can show him how sexy he is by wearing a teddy to bed.

If you *do* have a problem with his ever-expanding forehead, first admit it to yourself. Avoid dropping little hints like "Elton John's wig looks great" or leaving bottles of Rogaine on the bathroom counter. He's not going to be fooled, and he'll resent your attempts to tell him what to do—no matter how subtly you do it. Instead, ask yourself what *really* bothers you about your man's hair loss. Is he less attractive to you? Do you feel ashamed of him around your friends? Does he remind you of your dad? Does his receding hairline remind you that he's aging, and that scares the daylights out of you? Be honest. Get specific. You don't have to tell him what you uncover, but it's important for *you* to know the truth. Once you do, you can deal with the *feeling*. You can't change the reality of his hair loss, but you can work on your own fear of abandonment, insecurity, sense of love. You can figure out why his hair loss feels like a reflection on *you*. It isn't, but if it feels like it is, that's a sign that you might want to spend less time looking at the top of his head, and more time looking inside your own heart.

Regardless of where they fit on the evolutionary scale, for most males appearance serves as proof of virility. Human male plumage may be subtler or less inherent than an animal's (few wolves can shop for a niftier pelt; our guys have options), so knowing how to interpret what you see is crucial in identifying Alpha males. It's a sort of "secret handshake" among men. Believe me, guys know how to "read" one another's appearance, "hear" what the other guy is broadcasting by what he wears.

Males use clothing as a way to *announce* status when they have it, and camouflage the fact that they're losing it when they feel they are. Men understand the secret language of cuff links and Rolexes, can spot a well-tailored suit or an expensive tie. Women react more instinctively. They like it when their guy looks good, but few women understand what's really going on underneath a man's outerwear.

When it comes to "reading" a man's appearance, it's helpful to understand that adult men's clothes have a certain hierarchy. Take blue jeans—the uniform of the workingman—originally made of indestructible cloth from Nîmes, France (that's where the name *denim* comes from: *de Nîmes,* meaning from Nîmes). Sailors and railroad workers and farmers wore "de Nîmes" when they had to do dirty work that would ruin any other clothes. Blue jeans worn by men are now most often worn by *younger* males; they emphasize the penis and buttocks—primary and secondary sexual characteristics. A workingman's blue jeans are saying, "I may not have monetary power, but baby, I sure have animal magnetism and I'm not afraid to flaunt my manhood." Workingmen are the "can-do" guys who trumpet their raw virility front and center for all the world to see. And when Joe Junior Exec from down the hall shows up in jeans on Casual Friday, you'd better believe that he's sending a message to both the young women and the old men in the office.

A number of years ago I was visiting my mom in Denver and got a call from a friend I'd known when my daughter was young who invited me to Boulder for a party. All I had with me was a little silk dress and heels, which I arrived in, and was promptly whisked off to a town just above Boulder that had no electricity—

an old-fashioned sort of mining town done up in a baby-boomer, hip style, incredibly chichi, with everyone in blue jeans but me. One guy there was the great-grandson of an original Supreme Court justice, another was a governor's son. They were being sort of "fake" hicks; I was one of the few "real" hicks there since I'd grown up in the area (in blue jeans, I might add), and here I was dressed in silk and heels! It struck me how far the original concept of jeans as a "workingman's" outfit had come.

Uniforms, worn by cops, military officers, doctors, among others, are announcing that the men who wear them are members of the brotherhood, part of a pack. These men have other men to watch their backs, to care for their women should anything happen to them. They have proven loyalty and discipline. Uniforms represent different levels of authority. They're saying, "We're all the same, but we're not." It's insider information. If you know how to interpret the uniform, you can identify the Alpha males. If not, everyone appears to have the same status. Most uniforms are designed to emphasize and advertise male strength—broad shoulders, narrow waists. They announce to females, "I can support you," and to males, "My pack can beat the daylights out of you." Instead of being about raw sexuality, uniforms are about authority and solidarity.

Suits indicate a certain solidarity as well. A *boy's* first pair of long pants is his initiation into manhood. Typically worn by older men, suits are saying, "I am replacing brawn with brains." It's time to achieve status though the pocketbook, not the bulge in the pocket. Suit pants are loose, the jacket covers the genitals. Suits neutralize the male sex. They camouflage the male organ. The only remnant of sexuality is the *tie*, which is symbolic of the male penis—complete with two little "testicles" on each side when knotted! And each morning, "the suits" voluntarily strangle their sexuality by tying a noose around their necks. How much more Freudian can you get?!

Men know how to "read" a suit. They can size up a competitor by the cut of his jib, literally the *trappings* of his success. For instance, most men realize that the number of buttons on a jacket sleeve indicate how expensive the jacket is. The more buttons, the ritzier the suit. (Supposedly this came from Napoleon, who, in an effort to stop his soldiers on sentry duty from wiping their noses on the sleeves of their uniforms, ordered buttons sewed on everybody's cuffs.)

The best suits have discreet interior labels that can be flashed by the wearer if desired, but men understand that powerful men needn't flash labels at all. Label identification is for males who feel power*less* and need an external "proof" of virility.

I first learned about men and labels when I was a grad student in Boston struggling to put myself and my husband through school. One of my jobs was to go into welfare homes and counsel families. Since I was broke, I would buy the cheapest brand of everything: food, clothing, shoes. I noticed, however, that guys from poor families would pay top dollar for designer labels. They'd have the goods while I wore the off-brands, even though theoretically I was financially better off. My identity was not dependent upon a label, but if you feel impotent, you can use trappings as camouflage. An expensive label announces, "I'm as good as you," which is crucial especially if you feel you're really not.

Exterior, visible labels as a fashion statement, particularly among the young and disenfranchised, is an obvious continuation of the need to appear powerful and the amazing ability of the human species to arbitrarily assign status and value to externals. In some ways, humans are most able to escape their biological destinies—but not completely! Tommy Hilfiger, Fila, Hugo Boss all wear their names literally on their sleeves. "Fashion" as we know it targets teenagers, women, people who have historically been viewed and view themselves as second-class citizens who don't feel very important. "Loud" labels help them feel important because they are symbols of what others deem important.

Ever wonder why . . .

. . . pimps wear such flashy clothes and jewelry? They are *separating* themselves from the pack, saying, "I'm more manly than you because you have to support women and women support *me.*" They are announcing to everybody that they are literally beyond the pale. Their dress identifies them as more manly than "the Man." They can make a mockery of what mainstream America says is "manly" because they do the most "manly" thing of all: They totally *control* women. Women make them rich, and they want to flaunt that fact as obviously as possible. You have to *pay* to have access to my woman, buster. I can break all the rules.

The high end of the sartorial pecking order is the tuxedo. It's worn on special occasions, it's black and white, it covers a man's tail and penis, it makes his shoulders look big. In tuxedos, every man is an equal at that moment. Typically, tuxedos are *rented*, so they're not a reflection on the size of a man's wallet. They unite men at an event—wedding, retirement party, fraternal gathering. A tuxedo is a way to suspend competition, allow men to relax and have fun and be freed from the urge to compare, contend, and control.

The *low* end of the sartorial pecking order is the bathing suit, or more specifically, the *Speedo* bathing suit. Emotionally, a man might as well be naked. Imagine going to the beach with a man and his boss and watching the two of them strip down to Speedos. *Yikes.* There's nowhere for either guy to hide. The Alpha male has no camouflage, which favors the younger guy. But the younger guy risks retaliation from an Alpha who is more powerful. Hmmm . . . perhaps that's why you don't see too many company picnics at the beach!

WILD THINGS

Q. *Chameleons deliberately change their color to:*
  a. Blend into their surroundings and avoid danger.
  b. Attract a mate.
  c. "Disappear" in the middle of a fight.

A. *None of the above.* The chameleon's color change is one of the myths of the animal world. While it's true that chameleons change color in the face of danger, or as a result of exposure to light and heat, a chameleon can't deliberately change its color to match its environment. The color change is involuntary and is as unlikely to match the surrounding environment as to match its color. A chameleon's color change, like a male human's hairline, body shape, age spots, color sense, color *blindness*, is beyond his control. Acceptance—and focusing on interiors more than exteriors—is a much more effective way of making everybody feel better about themselves.

Q. *A moose's antler size is most evolutionarily effective as a:*
    a. Sexual stimulant to the female.
    b. Weapon against other combatant males.
    c. Combat deterrent.

A. *Combat deterrent.* The bigger the moose's antlers, the more *unlikely* it is he'll have to do battle with another male who wants his females. As a result, the more *likely* it is he'll survive to impregnate several females and propagate the species. Just as it is among human males, studly appearance isn't as much about alluring women as it is about keeping other males *away.* It's about competition among *males;* females are the prize, and certainly necessary for reproduction, but the real driving force behind a male and his "plumage" is keeping other males off of his turf, away from his woman, and far away from a battle for Alpha male.

Boys to Men

A BOY'S PLUMAGE becomes an issue at puberty. Before adolescence when hormones start acting up and exciting interest in girls, boys are mostly concerned with the size of their *skateboard* or who has the coolest video game. A preoccupation with appearance is considered unmanly *before* puberty and a bit of a mixed bag afterward.

Once puberty hits a *girl* upside the head, she gets a growth spurt, breasts, and attitude. Boys of the same age are left in the dust. Most thirteen-year-old boys are still short, with high voices, soft, unmuscled skin, and hairless chins and genitals. At this age, clothing is about covering up, fitting in, fading into the scenery. For most boys, adolescence is about feeling shame, being awkward, and trying to hide it from everyone—sibs, friends, enemies, teachers, parents, and the dreaded Amazon sitting next to him in homeroom. Life is further complicated by unexpected erections in class, the cafeteria, and while watching the Miss America pageant and *The Little Mermaid* on TV. It's about feeling out of control—for *years*.

Most boys don't start getting height, coordination, and baritone until high school. That's when they're finally taller than the girls. They have stubble and hair down there. They are Alpha males in training. The want to strut their stuff and show other potential Alphas that they have what it takes. By high school, most boys become more interested in how they look. Fashion becomes both a way of fitting in and a way of standing out—both an identification with the group and a statement of personal style.

Men in general and teenage boys in particular have bought into the ludicrous notion that they reach their sexual peak at eighteen, whatever that's supposed to mean. Guys believe that the way their penis behaves at eighteen is the way a "virile" man's penis ought to behave at any age. He ought to have erections at will and ejaculate within forty-five seconds. Hard (if you'll forgive the term) to imagine any woman who would find this "quick-draw McGraw, anything turns me on" approach as sexy. But guys have convinced one another that this "penis-centric" view of the universe in which their definition of a man rests on a six-inch (?) section of his body is valid. If the "little guy" doesn't perform the way his owner thinks it should, he feels like they're both "losing it." It's the beginning of the end. At eighteen! *Yikes!* You can see why guys feel so serious about controlling *something* in their lives.

Talk about a short shelf life: Nearly as soon as a young man recognizes his sexual potential, he fears losing it. Since a male's masculine identity is attached to his sexual potency, he spends his adult life compensating for losing what he views as his virility, his very manhood. And if you want to talk compensation—think, er, *compensation* (money), fast cars, corner offices, big guns, John Deere tractors, Hair Clubs, loose clothes, Harleys, wanton women, Super Bowl Sundays, and trophy wives. Men spend their grown-up years doing whatever it takes to prove they're as studly as they would have liked to have been as teens. The irony—when you've got it, you can't get it, and once you can get some, you're losing it.

Once a man's penis doesn't work the way he thinks it ought to, he reaches for what he figures will work next best as an aphrodisiac: the dynamic duo, *money and power.* His hairline may recede, his penis may droop, his knees may ache, his eyes may waver and water, but as long as he can *show me the money,* he's Aristotle Onassis. Most men believe that they best be prepared for the day when their penis won't stand up and salute on demand by accumulating a comforting bank account or a large piece of land or a whopper of a promotion to get the girl and keep other guys away. So their lives—their clothes, their *looks*—are all geared toward progressively covering the penis, while successively displaying other status symbols, like a pin-striped suit, a bountiful harvest, a new store, a Samsonian head of hair, and, of course, a fabulous, expensive, luxurious, silken *tie.*

Working It Out Together

WOMEN MAKE the mistake of thinking their men dress to please (or displease) *them*. The exact opposite is true. Men dress fundamentally for other *men*. (Oh, I know they'll say it's all about comfort—but you'll never catch him in a comfortable long skirt or soft, fuzzy see-through bathrobe.) Understanding that his appearance is one way he competes with other males is the first step in not taking a man's wardrobe personally.

A fifty-eight-year-old woman named Helen called my program to complain that her *ex*-husband had suddenly taken an interest in his appearance. "I begged him for years to stop dressing like a slob, but he wouldn't. Now that it's time to attract some bimbo, he's wearing all the great clothes I gave him!"

Helen fell into a trap many women do. She *begged* her husband to stop looking like a *slob*. She treated him like a child and insulted him at the same time. Her husband's refusal to comply was saying, "You can't tell me what to do." And he was right; she couldn't. It wasn't until *he* had the desire to fluff up his own feathers that he started wearing Calvin Klein instead of Kmart. After his divorce, Helen's ex wanted to prove to himself and other men that his manhood was still intact. How do you do that? One good way is by attracting a cute little chickadee. It's a way of keeping younger, stronger males at bay by proving he can get the girl. His penis may not perform the way it used to, but a trophy wife is literally that, a *trophy*, showing all those young lions he can still reproduce, and can compete against them and *win*.

When a man cross-dresses, women often mistakenly take it personally, too. Cross-dressing or transvestism or gender dysphoria (meaning "discomfort") is wearing clothes of the opposite sex for sexual excitement. It's not inherently gay, dangerous, or antisocial. In fact, most cross-dressers are middle- and upper-class white heterosexual professional males with high intelligence. Women with men who cross-dress needn't shame them; instead, they can ask that it be done in private and that their clothing not be appropriated. When you think about it, what's the harm as long as he doesn't wear your favorite things?

If a woman feels her man is sartorially handicapped, rather than treating him like a ten-year-old going out for his first pair of long pants, try making him feel sexy *as is*. Once a guy feels sexy, he feels invincible. Feeling invincible means *he* doesn't have to prove anything to anybody. He can let his guard down and risk changing his plumage. Plus, most guys would rather eat shards of glass than go shopping for clothes. Women spend hours roaming through the mall; guys are in and out in five minutes. Helen would have been wise to quietly buy new clothes for her husband, hang them in his closet, then let it go. Hovering over a man while he fumbles with buttons only makes him feel like a child. Letting him dress *himself* makes him feel like the adult male he is.

Understanding what a man is trying to communicate with his appearance is crucial in truly understanding him. He may be saying, "I'm unique" or "I'm rich" or "I'm so secure in myself I don't need to prove anything" or "I'm scared." He may be saying, "I'm losing my hair and I'm freaking out" or "I want everyone to see how manly I am, so I'll only wear tight jeans" or "I'm going to prove my wife can't push me around by staying fat when she wants me to be thin." Deciphering the message beneath his image can help men and women appreciate one another more. Dealing with the underlying issue can help men and women get closer to one another. By understanding that *everyone's* appearance is communicating something to the outside world, and figuring out what their men are trying to "say" to other *men*, women can stop judging men by their looks and start looking at what really matters: what they're wearing on the *inside*.

QUANTUM

MEN

WOMEN

MEN	WOMEN
Don't believe that clothes make the man.	Don't dress your man—it makes him feel unmanly, cut off from the pack.
Understand that clothes are camouflage; practice baring your soul more (at least to yourself) and feeling the need to cover your body, back (or ass) less.	Sincerely find something to compliment about his appearance daily.
Look in your eyes (not your beard) at least once a day in the mirror while shaving.	Plan a week's worth of your outfits in advance so you wake up and don't think about your clothes.
	The next time you go out on a date, dress for comfort instead of sexuality and see how it feels.
	Look at yourself naked in the mirror each day.
	Go to a strip show or a gym locker room to see that all sorts of sizes and shapes make up the female form.

LEAPS

Nine

Going for the Kill
Men and Money

A DOMINANT MALE chacma baboon hunts alone and eats alone, sharing his kill only after he's had his fill. Even when the entire baboon troop bands together for a group hunt, the dominant males eat first—before females and baboon babies, and certainly before any adolescent males who have their eye on the top rung of the social ladder. Food, in the animal kingdom, is *currency*. It's hunted and collected and sometimes hoarded. Food is how animals survive and how some dominant males prove their superiority. Even in a pride of lions where the lion*esses* do the dirty work of bagging a zebra or wildebeest, the dominant males are the first to move in for a meal. The most important animals get the most, best, tastiest food; all others are left to gnaw on the bones.

The hunt—going for the kill—is all about strong versus weak. Rarely will an animal attack his *equal*. Instead, predators venture forth in search of small, weak, injured, inattentive, isolated prey.

It's not personal, it's efficient: Attacking a mama's cute, cuddly cubs isn't mean or cowardly or cruel—it's *survival*. It's adding currency to the vault, and the animal with the largest stash wins.

The Human Animal

FOR MOST MEN, money is life's report card. Every other, every earlier scorecard counts for nothing. The human male animal with the largest stash, greatest wealth, most wampum wins. In our society, money is power, status, independence, choice, lifestyle, and authority. Money is a symbol of strength, while its opposite, poverty, by definition defines second class and implies weakness and subordination. It's the Golden Rule incarnate: He who has the most gold rules. Hey look, don't get mad at me—I didn't make the rules, I'm just the messenger. And the message is: Money is sexy!

Aristotle Onassis was short, really short, but when asked about his lack of physical stature, he casually noted that when standing on his wallet he was as tall as almost any man he knew. That doesn't matter so much anymore, you say. Well, if movies exemplify a cultural dream or ideal, then the movie *Indecent Proposal* is the perfect illustration of how men use money to flaunt their sexuality, status, and dominance over other men. Remember how Robert Redford uses his wealth to continuously reinforce Woody Harrelson's sense of his own inadequacy? Though Redford's apparent goal is to get the girl (if only for a while), the battle is really between the two *men*; Demi Moore is just the prize. Because the Harrelson character believed what most American men believe in their gut—that money *does* make the man—he psyched himself right out of a relationship with the woman he loved.

A number of years ago, I read a journal article about an "innovative" approach to the treatment of depression. The article told of a man who had sought therapy because he was depressed following the loss of his job. The family was temporarily supported by his wife, who had been a nurse and who went back to work. During the sessions, the therapist explored his patient's relationship with his father and his self-image, but mostly they worked on getting him emotionally together enough to apply for another job (therapy as career counseling). He talked about how depressed he felt being home all day with the kids, without working, and how bad he felt about not making money. After a couple of months, and a good job offer, he was back on track and his depression had "miraculously" lifted. He felt elated and thankful. As a footnote, the therapist noted that after his client had been working for a while, he returned to therapy with a new and furious complaint: His wife had refused to quit her job after he got his. He wanted her to return home where she "belonged," but she refused to return to the same situation that had so profoundly depressed him.

Money and work were not only the badges of courage for him, but were also part and parcel of his self-definition. When they went away, so did his sense of self. Hence, his depression and inability to function. Interestingly enough, he was able to see this phenomenon as not only personal, but crucial, and decided it had no relevance to his *wife's* sense of herself. Her working actually threatened him because she could now do his "thing," i.e., make money.

Look, a man without a job is really a man without a self-definition. For most men, their job is like their *skin*—it holds everything else together. Work and money is the outward presentation of who he is. So, Tarzan, if you're not working right now, it's going to be a scary time. Instead of ignoring the fear, it can be used as a motivator to look at options and really decide what you *want* to do. Get out a pad and pencil and make three lists. First, write down all the things you're good at (which may or may not have anything to do with what you were doing before). Then list what you love to do (which may *not* be what you're an expert at right now). Finally jot down what you've always wanted to do. Use my magic wand. It doesn't have to be practical—you may have always wanted to play center for the Boston Celtics even though you're five-two. That's okay, write it down. What you're doing is distilling the essence of what you want so you can examine all the possibilities. Wanting to play for the Celtics may mean you like vigorous physical activity, being around men in a competitive atmosphere who view every day as a new start with a lot of unpredictability and travel. If that's the case, sales may be a great job for you (maybe even selling sporting goods or advertising time in sporting events) instead of some managerial position.

Being out of work means you have time to figure out what you want to do next. While you may feel thrown for a loop, it's important not to be undone or consider yourself less of a man or feel you have to suck it up and not be bothered. Being bothered is perfectly okay, coin of the realm even, but you don't have to be overwhelmed or destroyed by the experience.

If your Tarzan is out of work, Jane, this is not the time to mother him or be his therapist; he's already feeling impotent, like a boy, like he has no power. This is not the time to organize his job search for him or bug him about it. Finding a new job may take him longer than you think. Just because he's reading the newspaper for two hours each morning doesn't mean he's not thinking about getting a job every minute. Men understand that getting a good job takes time and patience; they also understand how frightening unemployment is for a family. Calling his attention to it is unnecessary. Instead, ask him, "Is there something I can do to help?" and then back off.

You may have to deal with your own fears if he's the mainstay of the family. *Both* of you may view his joblessness as "unmanly" right now. Be careful that your fears don't end up making you mother him. He'll feel even less manly than he already does (which is why guys often become babies when they're sick—it's the only time they can legitimately be invalids, literally *invalid* as moneymaking, aggressive Alpha males, without losing their manhood). If you're terrified about not having enough money, get a job yourself, or a higher-paying one, to ease some of the financial worries.

Money is a powerful *emotional* force. All its value is psychological and symbolic, since in and of itself, money is green, grungy, inert rag paper (barely worth the paper it's printed on) that just lies there. But money is also symbolic of the very essence of manhood—the ability to protect and provide for the pack, and keep the wolf from the door. And it has always been thus: Cavemen brought pelts back to warm their cavewomen, American Indians decorated themselves and their squaws with wampum, farmers fed their families and traded with crops and cattle, 49ers rushed to California for gold, and South African men mined diamonds to trade with the world.

For most of human history, *only* men could inherit or pass on wealth (a dowry was considered a way for the father of the bride to literally "pay back" the bridegroom for taking on the financial responsibility of his daughter) and, in fact, women were considered currency. Which is why women working in large numbers (especially at "male" jobs or well-paying, high-status ones) really upsets the old apple cart as well as the psyche. In spite of statements to the contrary, what's threatening is *not* proximity, the distraction of a well-turned ankle in the workplace, or the bruising of the good ol' boy network: It all hits the fan when women can make as much *money* as their men. Women who have money have power. Men who have women with money lose some of their power over *her*. A woman with money can say "No" and "Good-bye," which are two threatening words to any man.

Ever wonder why . . .

. . . husbands give their wives "pin money"? In the Middle Ages, husbands gave their wives silver pins as a gift for the New Year. In time, guys started giving their wives pin *money* instead (even then men hated to shop!), which eventually became an allowance for household stuff. What began as a gift became a *budget;* what was once a way to honor women became a means to control them by controlling their spending.

We know that there is an enormous disruption in a marriage—particularly sexually—when a woman begins to make more money than her man. Even some highly evolved couples freak out when traditional male/female roles are knocked upside the head. A friend of mine worked out what I thought was the perfect arrangement. She was aggressive and successful at work; he loved children and being home and was bored by his job. So she went to Wall Street and made the big bucks while he raised the kids and made cookies. To their astonishment and chagrin, they couldn't get beyond the sense that he was diminished because *she* was bringing home the bacon and *he* was cooking it.

The abstract *idea* of Mr. Mom was one thing; the gut reaction was quite another. The marriage floundered and she admitted that she felt her husband was less of a man because he had no income; her husband felt he was less of a man, too. And even less expectedly, both felt she was less *feminine* as well. Sad but true, but whether it's Hollywood, TV, or murder mysteries, women who make gobs of money are viewed as dangerous ball-busters and bitches. Their male counterparts are praised as being lions, Young Turks, leaders of the pack. Women may have achieved a limited degree of financial parity in the past fifty years (hey, sixty-seven cents on the dollar is better than nothing), but emotional parity moves at the same speed as glaciers.

Once again, size matters. In the new world, it's the size of his paycheck. In a country without aristocracy, money is royalty. Look at the great philanthropists in this country, the Carnegies, Mellons, Rockefellers, Kennedys—past the first generation no one looked too carefully at how the money got made. Just look at the heft of it. Today young men in the inner city aspire to emulate wealthy, powerful "role models" who are often drug dealers and pimps. How the money is made is secondary to its existence: Cash to flash is blinding. Big men have big bank accounts. That's the way it is in the modern jungle.

Ever wonder why . . .

. . . men won't discuss their salaries with one another? Men understand that you're worth exactly what you can get. When a man tells another man his salary, he is saying, "This is how much I value *myself.*" Women assume that their salaries reflect how much their *bosses* value them. Men take it much more personally. A small salary (and every man thinks he's worth *more*) is the equivalent of having no guts. Having no guts means you're wimpy, and being wimpy means you're not manly. And not being manly is something no man ever wants to admit— especially not to another guy. I actually just saw a play, *Hurrah at Last,* by Richard Greenberg, in which a man would rather drop his pants and show his genitals than admit how much money he makes.

Money is power. Period. Which is why a man would prefer to *make* it rather than inherit it. What's more manly, a self-made millionaire or a rich kid riding his daddy's coattails? Guys who literally *make* their way in the world are considered studs, cowboys, he-men. Proving that you can go man-to-man in the jungle and pummel the competition is what makes most guys feel like pounding their chests and announcing, "I'm king of the world!" It's what turns most women on, too.

Inherited wealth has given way to the "Stupid Grandson" theory of life: The first generation grows up in poverty because most men don't get their really great idea until they are adults. Quite often, they were struggling before that, not fitting in, working in a job they didn't like. Once their genius surfaces, they are adults, and getting in on the ground floor means they can make scads of money, but they have to wait. The second generation—the sons of the previously poor Alpha males—grow up in their father's shadow and tend to be very conservative and intimidated by Dad. The son won't make great financial leaps forward, but it's sort of like a solid mutual fund—he'll slowly build wealth. The problem is the third generation: the grandson. He grew up in wealth, he's intimidated by the legend of his grandfather, so he tends to demean his conservative father. He views his father as a wimp and his conservatism as fear. The grandson grows up with a sense of entitlement, scoffs at a conservative approach, has no idea what his grandfather was really all about since he knew him only as a larger-than-life figure . . . and he'll run a company into the ground. Men who inherit wealth feel emasculated their entire lives. They have to prove they are manly one way or another, often acting out sexually or risking their lives by driving too fast or being careless in other ways.

Accumulating wealth is how Alphas-in-training become leaders of the pack. And often, the hunt is more thrilling than the kill. Earning money feels better than having it. *Being* rich means the chase is over, the competition has cooled. *Getting* rich means the hunt is on—the hounds are out, the trumpets sound, the horses are fresh, and the adrenaline is pumping. Which is why men gamble more than women.

Money is a very different commodity for men than it is for women. Money is a man's language, passport, and badge of honor.

It's literally "bread"—the staff and stuff of life (don't go too Freudian on me here!). The difference between how men and women view money is never more evident than in gambling. Men gamble in Vegas, in the stock market, on the job. They risk losing money because most believe they can make it again. They can be Donald Trump and start all over. They can get back in the race. It's also why guys who inherit money are often so chintzy—even though they *have* the big bucks, they don't know how to *make* it if they lose it all. Instead of feeling financially secure, they feel vulnerable. Interestingly enough, one of the largest groups of new gamblers, especially in casinos, are *widows.* (Hmmm . . . the money is now all theirs, although traditionally women have taken their chances on *men.*) Both men and women gamble in their area of "expertise" and competence. Men gamble with their wallets, women gamble with their hearts. Both are using the coin of their realm.

Acquiring money is not only how men compete with one another, it's how they attract busty young flesh and prove whose is bigger. Men with money are society's power brokers; women with money are society's threats. Look at the differences: Women who marry men for their money are considered trophy wives; men who marry women for their money are considered gigolos. Martha Raye was presumed to have lost her marbles for having a young man around; Cary Grant, Milton Berle, and Fred Astaire were thought to be virile for having young wives. No company executive ever told a man they would pay him more because he had children to feed, yet women are routinely paid less or are the first to be laid off because bosses assume they have someone else to take care of them.

When I was a fifteen-year-old high-school senior, my parents won a trip to Bermuda. I'd already been accepted to Rice University and was planning to start in the fall. The night before my parents left for Bermuda, my dad showed me where his will was and told me that if my parents' plane should crash, I was not to go to college. Instead, he wanted me to get a job and put my *brothers* through school. (At the time, one of my brothers was ten and the other was five.) Besides the fact that the only possible way I could afford to send them to college was to go to college myself and get a good job, the message was clear: It's crucial for *boys* to succeed in life. And the way they succeed is through an education that can earn them *money.* My function was to ensure their success. Dad was completely sincere in his belief that the male makes the money, and the female does whatever it takes to help him make the money. It wasn't personal, just alarming!

As with everything else, kids learn about money from Mom and Dad. Boys, in particular, are taught what money means by watching Pop, since men still hold most of the family purse strings. Even though moms pay most of the bills, dads bring home most of the money. Parental interaction over the almighty dollar influences kids long after they're grown and have credit-card debt of their own.

Once, a caller told me his parents had fought over money so often at the dinner table that even today he can't sit down for a meal without worrying about his stock options. How, then, to give both boys and girls a more balanced, less stomach-churning, less gender-based view of a dollar that is relevant without being Almighty? The answer lies in separating *emotion* from money and dealing with the green stuff in black-and-white terms. First, this means getting very specific about how much you need to make ends meet, and how you can earn the dough. Second, nothing helps you put money in perspective faster than earning and managing it *yourself.*

A friend of mine's mother used to say to her, "Remember: He who pays *says*." The person holding the purse strings is the person with the power. Jane, if you're totally supported by your husband, you're probably going to feel like a poor relation at one time or another—not to mention like a child whose daddy is doling out your allowance. If the two of you want the old-fashioned, male-based model of a marriage, so be it—but that precludes the millennium version of marriage as a *partnership.* You may have convinced yourself that caring for the kids and the house is holding up your end of the bargain, and it certainly is important, but kids grow up and leave, and the healthiest, happiest kids are raised by *both* parents. How are you going to convince him of that if you divide the world into inside and outside the house?

I admit up front I think the only way for women to convince men to shoulder that all-important parenting role is for women to be willing to shoulder some of the financial responsibilities. Women who don't have any experience in the working world often feel vulnerable and weak. Hey, *anybody* who's totally dependent upon another person for their survival feels vulnerable. If girls planned to work, they might be less dependent on boys for their sense of self. Raising kids is no longer a life's work. Kids leave at eighteen and parents live to eighty, which means an awful lot of adult life is going to be lived childless even if you're *really* fertile! Besides, just as teenagers feel good because someone is willing to pay for their time, so do we all. If your kids are young, start planning so that once they're in school, you can be, too. Or plan to be out there where the wind is free and so is the coffee! If you haven't a clue what to do, start working part-time *somewhere.* Exposure to other women in the workplace will open up your horizons. Go to the library. Talk to people. Look around and pick a job that looks fun. Being paid for the work you do can be exhilarating and empowering. Knowing you can care for yourself, and your family, makes you feel valuable and *powerful*.

JUNGLE GEMS

Understanding men and money means accepting these basic male notions:

+ *Money is power, status, and control.*
+ *Controlling money makes men feel manly.*
+ *Making money makes men feel studly.*
+ *Size (of the paycheck) matters.*
+ *Big paychecks make men feel like Masters of the Universe.*
+ *Money rules the world.*
+ *Women's money feels very different to both men and women.*
+ *Everyone's funny about money.*
+ *Men and women have very different philosophies about money.*

Tarzan, if you financially support your wife and feel that she spends too much money, take a closer look at what's going on. People who overspend are usually unaware of financial matters or acting out. Figure out which category your wife falls into. Is she angry? Is she trying to make you *pay* for something? If so, get to the bottom of the rage and the raging credit cards will calm down. More likely, you're the breadwinner in your family as well as the bill-payer and bank. Marriage is a corporation; even if you're CEO and your wife is head of the purchasing department, you're both responsible for the solvency of the company. It's crucial that you pay the bills *together*.

Sit down at the kitchen table, spread out the bills, look at the pay-check, and take it from there. Bringing her into the bill-paying process will be a reality check—perhaps for *both* of you.

Once you do this, it will be clear whether there's enough money to go around. If there is, ask yourself why you resent her spending the excess. If there isn't, ask her where she feels you can both make up the difference. In any budget, it's important to have enough money to pay for necessities, as well as a little left over for some fun stuff. Money ought to be used for pleasurable activities and purchases as well as the electric bill. Once you pay the bills together, and you both have a clear idea where all the money goes each month, accusations can turn into solutions. Why blame some-one for spending too much when it's much more productive to figure out a way you *both* can get what you want?

Look, being broke stinks. Been there, done that, been awake night worrying about it, and couldn't afford the T-shirt I was wear-ing. But having money isn't the problem-solver most people think it is. There's a lot of evidence that lottery winners are more unhappy after they win than they were before! (See my last book, *Nine Fantasies . . .*) One of the reasons why it's a cliché is that it's true: Money really *doesn't* buy happiness, peace of mind, or love. If you're miserable without money, you'll find a way to be miserable with money, too. So if you feel stressed out about money, figure out what's upsetting you *right now.* Ask yourself why you feel that having more *things* will make you happy. If money is so tight that you can't pay the rent, get very specific about ways you can make enough of the green stuff to make ends meet. People in financial turmoil feel buried. Taking it one bill at a time helps. Looking for a job every day—even days when you don't feel like it—helps. Making an appointment with a credit counselor can also help you dig out from under an avalanche of bills. The important thing is to take *action.* Moaning only makes money matters worse; making a *move* is the first step in making yourself feel better.

Removing the emotional impact of money reduces it to a manageable size. When money *doesn't* mean love, security, power, status, and control, it can become what it was originally intended to be—a means of *barter.* I want something from you, you want something from me, let's exchange two things that we agree are of equal value. And when it comes to raising your kids, taking emotion out of the financial equation teaches both male and female kids that money *doesn't* buy happiness, that hiring somebody to do the work you hate to do is a *good* use of funds, that loving your job is more important than loving your paycheck, and that a person's value goes far beyond what's in his or her wallet. That's why I'm a big believer in allowances and jobs. Tasks should be assigned a monetary value. I'm not suggesting that kids should be paid for brushing their teeth or making their own beds, but the familial chores—like cleaning the toilets or taking out the trash—ought to be valued. That's the way the world works, so why not get comfortable with it? Children who understand that some tasks are deemed more valuable than others will learn to value themselves, and what they do, more generously. Once a household task has a particular value, kids who don't want to do their chores can pay a younger brother or sister to do them for them, and figure out ways to make money that make more sense to them, like baby-sitting or a paper route.

Learning the lesson of value is crucial for kids, beginning with valuing themselves. Which is why I'm also a firm believer in adolescents' having a job. I don't care if they're mowing lawns, shoveling snow, working at McDonald's, or selling Furbies over the Internet, a paying job is the ultimate statement that somebody who doesn't love you *values* what you do. Most adolescents feel that nobody cares if they live or die. A job is proof that somebody *does* care; somebody does value the teenager enough to *pay* them. They exist beyond the parental unit because people who don't know them or love them are still willing to prove they value them by shelling out the greenbacks.

Money is power. Kids feel powerless. Money helps kids gain a sense of their own worth in the world. Teaching kids to *esteem* themselves (the word *esteem* comes from the Latin *aestimare*, meaning "to fix the price or value of") helps them put money—and everything else—in perspective.

Money, per se, is a relatively modern concept. Since earliest times, animals and humans have hoarded resources and traded them out for favors, women, allies, or hot sauce. Early North African cultures around 6000 B.C. traded *cattle* and later used grains and various crops as "cash." It's even thought that writing was developed in Mesopotamia as a way of keeping track of who traded what to whom. Early banks were established to accept grain and cattle "deposits." The Chinese character for "money" was initially a brightly colored cowrie shell. Trobriand Islanders traded shells as currency at potlatches and introduced the concept of conspicuous consumption into anthropology, resonating with later Thanksgiving feasts, Super Bowl parties, and Ed McMahon.

It wasn't until 700 B.C., in Lydia, Turkey, that the first coins were used. They were made from a blend of gold and silver and were easier to cart around than a cow. After that, coins started appearing in various parts of the world, made from all sorts of metals and mixtures. But not every culture used coins. The Chinese traded with pieces of deerskin, Arabs traded ivory, Far Easterners traded spices with Europeans, Portuguese traded guns for gold, slaves, and salt, and pelts were traded during the French-

Indian war. Even in relatively recent history, early Virginians traded tobacco leaves as currency, creating tobacco *certificates* in 1727 because handling the actual *leaves* was too messy.

Ever wonder why . . .

. . . the place where money is made is called the "mint"? It comes from the Latin word *moneta,* meaning "money." Specifically, the earliest "mints" were a "place of coining," because paper money wouldn't be invented for thousands of years. I know this because I grew up in Denver near the mint. (Does mint green refer to money or the stuff you put in juleps?)

"Money" is historically anything deemed valuable enough to trade. And *men,* almost exclusively, were the traders. Money matters were considered "indelicate," and actually handling coins and other forms of "cash" was a dirty business. In many societies, borrowing and lending money was restricted to certain people considered second-class citizens. Women were regarded as too clean and pure to mess around with such matters. A woman's fortune was almost entirely dependent upon her husband. Some marriages are still arranged by parents in India, Nepal, and some other parts of the world, with a "good" marriage considered a solid *financial* union. Marrying beneath your caste is out of the question. Until fairly recently, many wives all over the world knew *nothing* of their husbands' financial status. Men took care of every detail. It wasn't until women became widows that they began to understand how much money they had or didn't have. Ironically, when the *Titanic* went down and upper-class women and children were herded onto lifeboats, many survived to live a life of poverty or at least financial insecurity as, literally, their lifelines went down with the ship.

It's easy to see why so many women today view money as *security*, while their men view money as *control*. Men are historically programmed to treat money as their business . . . and their way of showing who's boss.

People who aren't funny about anything are funny about money. And heaven knows, when you put money together with sex—yowza, yowza! This isn't a new phenomenon: From preteen dating to final will and testament, men and women lock horns over money. Which shouldn't come as much of a shock if you've been paying attention. Many otherwise "liberated" women are turned off (if not downright offended) if a date asks to split the check. She feels dissed and he's considered cheap, less manly, less in charge. If he doesn't offer to pay at all, it's even worse. Money is male, money is penis, money is sperm—it's the stuff of life. Think about a dowry: It's one man saying to another man, "I'm willing to pay you to take her off my hands."

A highly successful thirty-three-year-old woman was offended when a surgical resident and potential beau asked her to pay for some of their dates. She wanted to know if she was overreacting. I said it seemed like they had such totally differing views of money and that they should talk about it immediately or shine each other on. The biggest cause of marital strife in first marriages is disagreements about money. The differing perspectives need to be uncovered and discussed before they can fester. Prenups (basically a dowry in reverse) are the latest attempt for men and women to come to grips with the intersection of love, sex, money, power, control, and commitment. Men aren't as intimidated by money-handling as women since they've been doing it so much longer. Typically men view money as a means for enjoying life, while women see money as a green life vest—a cushion against abandonment, something to save them from becoming a bag lady. He spends, she saves because opposites attract (then aggravate the daylights out of each other).

Since men have also traditionally been the breadwinners, they tend to have more of a proprietary sense about money. It's my paycheck, my mortgage, my car, my prerogative to spend as I see fit. Men also assume they'll die young. It's the James Dean philosophy of life: Live fast, die young, leave a good-looking corpse. Historically and actuarially this paranoia has a certain reality. Nowhere in that equation is: Work hard all your life so your wife can be a rich widow! Also, one of the major reasons men dread divorce is *finances.* Women don't want to be left alone; men don't want to be left penniless. Much of women's concern about men as commitment-phobics—Peter Pans who never want to grow up—likely has much more financial than sexual reality. Hey, a guy marries the wrong woman and he can lose at least *half* of everything he's earned. Divorce can be a financial wrecking ball for both sides.

When a man stops working, some of the biggest changes in the male/female dynamic occur. Even when a couple manages to get past the monetary shoals of dating, prenups, different styles of financial security, a roller-coaster stock market, and kids who don't repay loans, there's still *Retirement!* Some men literally die when they stop working. Money is their lifeblood. Without it, they lose their sense of manhood. For working women who retire (and we're only just beginning to have a large enough sample size to study), most have an easier time because they have often defined themselves by labels other than their jobs or careers.

What often happens when a couple retires is a complete role reversal: The *husband* wants to stay home and spend time with his wife; she wants to volunteer, work part-time, see her friends, spend time with her kids and grandkids. Since it's no longer about making money—presumably the investments have already been made, the social security and pension checks are coming each month—the power balance shifts. Yikes! How does a man define himself when he and his money can no longer practice the Golden Rule: He who has the gold *rules?* He's used to having his work and his family; she's used to having a varied social life. Without work— and without kids to provide for—a man's world can feel very small.

A thirty-eight-year-old woman called my program complaining about her fifty-two-year-old husband. "He's retired and he spends all his time with his adult kids," she said. I asked her if she was jealous and she said no. I asked if she wanted him to spend more time alone with her and she said no.

"So what's the problem?" I asked. She sighed and said, "He's spending all *my* money on them!" When I probed for more details, I found out that her husband had supported her for the nine years they'd been married. "Why won't you support him now?" I asked. She was not only flabbergasted, she was offended by the suggestion. Apparently "his" money was "hers," and making money of her own was out of the question. It's a dilemma I hear from a lot of couples. Old rules don't change overnight. For her, being a man meant *paying.* If *she* was paying, what did that make her, let alone him?

Resolving money disputes between two people is never easy, since money has symbolic meaning that varies so widely. Forcing a partner to adopt *your* way of dealing with dough is a great way to start an *argument*. You don't have to see eye to eye on every money matter. It's okay not to agree in this area. What you do have to do is figure out how to have enough money to pay the bills (which means *both* partners working or at least *both* deciding who works and *both* deciding how incomes are spent). It's crucial that no matter how little is left over, or even if you're both in the midst of pecuniary strangulation, that each of you have at least a small amount of discretionary income at the end of each month. Pay no attention to how your partner spends his or her discretionary income. That's literally none of your business.

WILD THINGS

Q. *When hunting, a large lion pride is more valuable than a smaller pride because:*

    a. More lions, more prey killed.

    b. There's safety in numbers.

    c. Several lions are needed to hold down the kill.

A. *Several lions are needed to hold down the kill.* Scientists have always believed that lions were social animals because a *group* improved their hunting success. That's true, but not because more lions mean more food. The opposite is true. The more lions in a pride, the less food each lion gets. Still, since hunting is hard work, lions need help pinning down prey once they catch it. The team effort ensures that lions get any food at all. When human survival is based on hunting or farming, the day-to-day survival of the family is improved because there are lots of helping hands even though the portions are reduced. Is it any wonder that in a postindustrial society, family size is shrinking?

Q. *An animal most often hunted and caught is:*

a. Young

b. Sick

c. Old

A. *All of the above.* Nature has created a way to make sure that the fittest animals survive. Hunters target the young, sick, and old, ensuring that healthy adults—the breeders— have the best chances of survival. This isn't unlike human retirement, where older individuals leave the workforce to make room for the younger bucks coming up. No wonder making money feels so powerful!

QUANTUM

MEN	WOMEN
Ask yourself what you'd do if you won the lottery; take one step in that direction.	Get a job if you don't have one.
Think about your options.	Plan on working for a large part of your life.
Figure out what you'd do if you had only one year to live.	Remember, money isn't about whose is bigger; it's about getting what you want.
Identify the first thing you'd buy if you had enough money; start saving for it.	Indulge yourself by buying something you see as a luxury that's only for you this week. Make sure it's something you can afford financially but emotionally have a hard time splurging on because it seems "selfish."

LEAPS

Ten

Women

THERE ARE A gazillion books about women—women's complaints about men, women's fantasies about men, women's fears about growing older around men, growing fiercer or more successful than men. Men have become the enemy. Hey, listen up: Men are neither the problem nor the solution for any woman, but yes indeedy, they do march to a somewhat different beat. Or more accurately, women seldom march—which results in troubled relationships and even the nutsy notion that males and females have different *planets* of origin, for heaven's sake!

As Bob Dylan said, the times they are *a-changin'*—the Berlin Wall has fallen, the cellular is ringing, test-tube babies are no longer newsworthy, and men and women seem angrier than ever before about what to expect from one another. Most of the old models of how to behave seem hopelessly outdated, with no clear pattern to take their place. This kind of change causes confusion, especially when it happens quickly.

Men are certainly different than they were millions of years ago, but male changes have been primarily evolutionary—slow and steady, with milestones having to do with either weather (Ice Age) or improved weaponry (Stone Age, Bronze Age) or the effective use of weaponry (Dynasties, etc.). One of the reasons things seem so dicey between men and women these days is that while men have been evolving slowly (hey, they had the power, what's the rush?), women have been making quantum leaps. Not because they are superior beings, but because they had little to lose and much to gain by changing the status quo.

This book is a call to arms (fleshy, not metal) to take a stand and understand that right here, right now on Mother Earth, evolution has brought us to the point where men and women want and need to understand one another and have the ability to accept one another for who we really are—if we could just sort out exactly who that is and how to do it without giving in or up. We've traveled through nine chapters about men together, so it's time to wrap up an understanding about men by talking about women, because nearly all the changes in the last fifty years have been instigated by the XX chromosomes gang.

Men have been placed in the historically unprecedented position of hanging on while women changed the rules. But shifting the balance of power requires fairness if the change is to be long term and beneficial rather than temporary and dangerous.

These days, women are adamant about demanding equal pay for equal work and an end to sexual harassment. They are calling for a sexual, economic partnership unprecedented in the history of marriage, complete with shared parenting and household responsibilities. Hey, you'll get no argument from me—it's all well and good unless these same women still consciously or unconsciously expect guys to do the calling, paying, driving, opening the door.

For if we still want men to be taller, richer, smarter, good providers and protectors, then we're still lookin' for Daddy. And Daddy has a lot more say over a child's life and choices than most women past the age of eight are willing to cede. It's not kosher for women to fight restrictions on their behavior while demanding unprecedented restrictions on their men—and you'd better believe that these expectations are restrictions. While most women are very clear about what they want, they are less aware of the inherent contradictions and restrictions they are simultaneously imposing on menfolk while hollering, "Don't fence me in, you male chauvinist pig!" You can see why men and women are so angry with one another.

The beginning of this humongous upheaval in male/female relations started in the 1920s, culminating with a bang (so to speak) in the late fifties, early sixties. When Margaret Sanger launched the American birth-control movement, the interaction between men and women grew more complex for women and certainly more confusing for men. What began as a way to help primarily New York Lower East Side immigrant women stop having more kids than they could afford to feed ended up in a little circular packet: the Pill.

Even though there had been previous tremors—women inheriting property, learning to read, getting the vote—when women were able to take charge of their reproduction, all hell broke loose. A woman with access to birth control has access to education, to the single life, to options, to the ability to just say *no* to pregnancy while saying *yes! yes! yes!* to sex on her terms and her schedule. Hey, guys just wanted to do what came naturally: mate and eat and work and watch football on Sunday afternoons. Suddenly their women weren't happy to have and care for the kids and the house and, oh yeah, *fill your own Doritos bowl!*

Men had been content with the previous status quo; women wanted to acquire status and knock quo upside the head. The male/female tug-of-war started in perhaps this most basic area of human animal life—reproduction—and spread like what many men might consider the ultimate sexually transmitted disease: the lust for equality. And we're still struggling.

IN THE JUNGLE

The female tamandua anteater carries her baby around on her back for *two years* before he's ready to go it alone. The baby hangs on to Mama while she forages for food or rips open an anthill and sticks her long snout inside. Having a toddler on your back is a bit burdensome, but hey, a girl's gotta do what a girl's gotta do. Who else is going to take care of the kid?

Female humans face a similar hurdle. Economically, work outside the home may be a necessity; emotionally, it may be just as crucial. But the tough question remains: Who takes care of the kids? Maternity leave, day care, split schedule, job sharing have allowed women to pursue both career and family with less than satisfying results—the Superwoman syndrome, the mommy track, job burn-out, and a general sense of dissatisfaction on everybody's part. Paternity leave hasn't exactly changed the world. Telling men to stay home and take care of the kids hasn't worked very well. Even guys who may sorta wanna try it worry about their careers, their buddies, and what their mother-in-law and the mailman and their wives *really* think of them. Hiring nannies is expensive and engenders a certain amount of both guilt and paranoia (should we install a nanny cam?); day care often fosters the same concerns augmented by the worry over whether the teacher is too busy with somebody else's kid. Strapping a baby into a backpack and schlepping off to work isn't very practical, so modern working moms are left praying for what allows their husbands to have both family and a career—a wife!

Okay, take a deep cleansing breath before going off the deep end here and let's look for practical solutions. Accept reality, number one. For most women, emotionally, raising children still feels like job one. Women get jobs, have careers, take over the company, but for the most part, they don't *define* themselves by what they do for a living. For most women it's still a Noah's Ark world. Pairing up to procreate still feels like survival, especially when coworkers discreetly ask about a love life with *either* sex and Mom keeps hinting and invitations to dinner parties seem tinged with a concern that somebody else's husband may be too willing to offer a ride home.

When I first became a psychologist, I did a lot of public speaking, partially because I was asked and partially because it was a good way of publicizing my practice at a time when there weren't a whole lot of women doing adult outpatient psychotherapy. After my speech, I was routinely asked, "Are you married?" which is asking "Are you straight?" since there was no man in evidence and I was supporting myself. That question was often followed by "Do you have children?" which was code for "Are you normal?" People still assume I don't have children even though I do, because the prevailing notion is that a woman has to give up being a mother if she wants to be successful at work.

I can't recall hearing a politician cry "family values" when *Dad* is at the office. The so-called "disintegration" of the family really means women aren't doing what "history" says they are "supposed" to be doing. As much as we like to think we've evolved, "women's work" is still frustratingly based on the age-old job of finding a man and bearing a child and figuring out how to fulfill ourselves professionally after we've fulfilled biological destiny.

Before we jump all over men, hollering about their insensitivity to housework and kids, women may have to rethink their priorities a bit. Doing housework isn't important, raising kids is. No one ever died or felt unloved because the furniture was dusty or the beds weren't made. Women who feel pulled in all directions might want to take a deep breath and focus on *options* rather than limitations: Hire someone to clean your house, or leave it dirty. Have fewer children, adopt kids later in life, work via fax and modem, get a night job, work part-time, flextime, organize neighborhood group baby-sitting, or invite Mom to move in. See if your husband can cut down on his hours as you beef up yours. Why not lobby for a twelve-month school year? Call other moms from your kid's school or around the neighborhood and brainstorm solutions to everybody's challenges.

I guarantee you that lots of other moms are feeling the same pinch.

IN THE LAIR

A female polar bear digs a den out of the previous year's compacted snow. She paws out an entrance tunnel and sometimes creates several rooms beneath the solid snowdrift. Inside, her cubs will be born and spend the winter. The mama bear keeps the den clean and tidy, covering her waste with fresh snow until she and her cubs emerge in the spring.

When it comes to hearth and home, female animals and *human* female animals are similar. In fact, until the last few years women's behavior hadn't changed much in the past 4 million years. On the one hand there is the immutable biological imperative: Females get pregnant and traditionally feed and care for their offspring. In some parts of today's world, a female can say no, but once she says yes, age-old practices swing into place. Even if the individual female feels a certain sense of rebelliousness, her body, her neighbors, her mom, and often her man will subtly or not so subtly remind her how things "are."

The norm is still that women are primarily responsible for what happens in the home (including the kids), while men go forth and are responsible for making most of the money. The rut isn't entirely societal. Many a female who adamantly demands that her man share all household and child-care duties builds a sort of "no-man's-zone" around the house by criticizing what a lousy job of diapering he does or cleaning up *after* he's already cleaned up. While on the one hand a guy feels that if he pitches in, rolls up his sleeves, and wears an apron, he'll be labeled "whipped" or wimpy, on the other hand he'll still be criticized for not cleaning well enough. His cooking stinks and he dresses the kids funny. She accuses him of purposefully doing a lousy job, of "acting out" his hostilities, and she may be right. But it's in that all-important area of parenting that it really hits the fan.

Today's father can't hold his daughters on his lap without the risk of being viewed as a child molester. Talk about a "no-win" situation! Women have not given men a satisfying role around the house, yet they decry the fact that men won't help out.

The easiest part of the solution begins with a definition: As I've said before, housework is *neither* men's work nor women's work—it's *house* work. Period. Women have bought the notion that the home is their domain and a clean house means they are a good woman or a worthy wife. Women interpret a man's help around the house as a sign that he values her, he doesn't consider her his slave or his maid. The fundamental problem with this thinking, though, is that it assumes housework somehow defines her. Women take it *personally* when a man doesn't empty the garbage. She feels insulted when he gets up from the dinner table without clearing his plate. But all she has to do is get up herself and join her husband in front of the TV, and as soon as the house runs out of clean dishes, somebody's going to wash them or buy paper plates or eat out or at least decide on some system that doesn't define love as disher-washer related.

When it comes to their lair, women need to understand that they impose *their* standards on a man without being conscious of the bullying nature of the whole ordeal. It's not fair or effective. Both men and women take grievous offense at being bullied. And let's face it—being defined by the shine on the kitchen floor is more than a little outmoded, and a kid in a perfectly pressed T-shirt says nothing about parenting, just laundry skills. When both men and women are willing to share, pay, or negotiate with one another or someone else to clean up at home, both can turn to more interesting, valuable, and important ways to disagree, show off, or demonstrate love as well as skill.

IN THE PRIDE

Female baboons hold the whole family together. A troop of baboons is a bunch of female relations. The oldest female holds the highest rank. Everybody bands together to care for the kids and bond with one another—including the males, who must first prove that they are willing to groom one another and make nice before they'll be allowed to make love. Within the baboon family, the *female* is king.

Most human families operate in the same manner, with females accepting the responsibility for most of the socialization in the family (with the exception of punishment). This responsibility appears so dominant that it is applied not only to young untamed offspring, but to older "untamed" mates as well. The female treats the male as an overgrown naughty child who doesn't know how to dress, act around authority figures (her father), or set limits (flirting with his secretary, swearing around the kids, getting drunk with the guys . . .). She further accepts the role of keeper of the external rules by remembering birthdays, and sending out holiday cards and gifts. Mommies plan birthday parties and teach their kids how to write thank-you notes. If a husband forgets his mother's birthday, the wife gets blamed. Kids with bad manners are thought to be poorly trained by their *mothers*.

When women spent all their time and energy being domestic and domesticating their unruly charges, this *might* have made sense. But as women leave the home to assume other roles and responsibilities, who takes over the job of finishing-school headmistress? Well, okay, buster, she says, "I'm working at the office, so you've got to pick up some of the slack." Only trouble is, women have been assuming these duties forever and men haven't.

Women want men to magically *think* like they do: caring for others' needs, juggling several balls at once, jotting down a grocery list while on hold with a client, swinging by the dry cleaner's on the way to work, sending flowers to Grandma on Mother's Day, scheduling the kids' checkup at the dentist and the pediatrician, and remembering to pick up Jane at soccer practice and Johnny at Little League. Guys have historically been allowed to be more focused, basic, even *primitive,* if you will. They get to think about work and sex and pastrami sandwiches. And that's all they *have* to think about. Which is where men and women run into trouble: Women get angry when men don't act like *women.*

The solution for women is to reach a man through his masculinity, not try to obliterate it. Once it is understood that guys haven't had the practice to be as proficient around the house or with the kids or with social matters, women can lighten up. Even if he happens to be somewhat talented domestically, it's unlikely he'll admit it except to show you "how it's done." Being good at "housework" makes him feel like he's Barbie, not Ken, a sissy, not a stud. He's simply not going to suddenly become "sensitive" just because you ask him to . . . or worse, *badger* him into it.

This doesn't mean a woman should be stuck with all the chores or with being a married single parent, it means women need to be very *specific* about what they want from men. Saying "I want you to help me with the kids" isn't good enough. Saying "I want you to take over the scheduling of the kids' doctors appointments" or "I want you to go to the supermarket every week" or "Here are the things that need to be done this week, do you want first or second choice?" or "You assign household tasks this week, I'll do it next week" is more effective.

If women are really being fair, they've got to give up some control and realize it's not kosher to ask a man to shop for food, then criticize the Twinkies he buys at the market. Women have to have the courage to stop taking everything that happens under their roof *personally.* Equality means giving up some of the *control* as well. True equality means meeting each other halfway.

IN THE PACK

Wild horses often form nonsexual bonds that appear to be crucial to their sense of well-being. Females and males groom, lick, and nuzzle one another, and gently nibble on one another's backsides. When horses are separated from their "friends," they often substitute another animal such as a cow or donkey, displaying the same bonding behavior. Domesticated horses have been known to nibble on the backs of their groomers in an attempt to re-create a relationship that's been lost.

Human females are justifiably renowned for their skill in relating to one another, sharing child-rearing, emotional intimacies, chores, and, for lack of a better word, "friendships." It almost goes without saying that women view themselves as superior to men in the friendship department. But when their men form friendships with women, they often feel threatened and suspicious and unwilling to entertain the notion of platonic relationships. They fear their main squeeze will be nibbling the backside of that friendly female. Or worse, he'll form a bond with another woman that is stronger than his bond with her. When it comes to friendships, women are simply not willing to extend to men the same leeway they expect men to extend to them. Women feel it's perfectly okay to have *male* friends, and it's okay for their men to have male friends, but *female* friends are theirs alone.

In a modern world, men are very likely to have female friends, since women are increasingly "invading" the places where men spend much of their time. More and more, the workplace offers an opportunity for a meeting of minds over mutual pursuits. As men and women work together, they find bases of esteem, respect, and even affection, which is the very definition of a friend. Women have platonic access to all sorts of men: trainers at the gym, physicians during office visits, pediatricians during exams, the kid's schoolteacher, the milkman, the postman. Women are used to having "platonic" powerful men in their lives, while traditionally, men have only had access to women of lower status: secretaries, housekeepers, wives. Now, when men are finally having relationships with women based on an *equality* of status (the basis of true friendship—no power differential), women feel threatened, fearing sex will rear its ugly head, which is a bit baroque.

Women either trust or don't trust their men. If you can't trust him, you shouldn't be with him. If you can, recognize that there have always been temptations and now there can be friendships. Period. If women want men to be more intimate, more open, more loving, more like their female friends, they must see that being threatened by the intimacy of *his* friendship with *her* is counterproductive. In fact, there is at least one "adultery" doctor who thinks that the risk of adultery *decreases* with male/female friendships because it allows for harmless flirtation and interaction without the traditional necessity of sex. It also allows a man to understand his woman better by knowing (*not* in the biblical sense!) and understanding another woman.

ON LOCKING HORNS

Most female animals don't even *have* horns to lock, which says a lot about the nature of fighting. In the wild, male animals lock horns with one another primarily to prove who's tough enough to get the girl. Most of the time, horns and bared fangs and chest pounding is a *deterrent* to an actual fight—literally a "show" of force to scare off the other guy. Some male animals do fight to the death, mostly to prove the point that "you definitely don't want to tangle with me or it could be a fight to the death—your death, bud." Female animals fight only when necessary—when somebody messes with their young. Otherwise, their attention is focused on finding food and caring for the youngsters and making sure everybody is warm and dry.

Conflict among human animals arises between men for all the ancient reasons—power, sex, and turf. But what separates humans from other animals is women's willingness to do the unthinkable of the animal kingdom: go head-to-head with her male for presumably the same stuff—power, sex, and turf. In a word, it's about *respect,* or why he came home late without calling or forgot their anniversary *again* or ignored her at the company party. When a woman locks horns with a man, blood is usually drawn since his imperative is to either back you off, slink away in defeat, or be prepared to fight to the death. Men have learned that fighting means winning and never, ever giving up. A wise woman tries to never enter the ring, not by manipulating to get her way but by effectively communicating rather than confronting. "Winning" her way means being smart, not tough, looking to the long term rather than treating every disagreement as a war to be won. This requires a *specific* awareness of exactly what you want *now*—the current context, the history of the problem as well as the relationship, and a shared perspective of future goals. You can see why it's so much easier but less profitable to fight than think.

In addition to knowing the immediate and long-term goals, the best way to walk away from a disagreement with both sides feeling that they "won" is to build on strengths instead of attacking weaknesses. I know generals would disagree. Go for the weak point! Vanquish and kill! But we're talking about an ongoing relationship here, not the spoils of war. Asking "How would you handle this if you were in my shoes?" or pointing to a specific action that upsets you allows both of you to focus on solving the problem by utilizing strengths and intelligence rather than weaknesses and brute force. Shifting the focus from criticism and defensiveness—making someone feel small and inept—to eliciting help with a problem is tapping into strength.

Specificity, with respect, is the clue here. Being treated like an equal partner—an adult—means resisting the temptation to cry, cajole, sulk, threaten, or manipulate. Think things through carefully, be specific about wants, and dare to ask for them without whining. Strategize straightforwardly rather than plot manipulatively; problem-solve rather than finger-point.

ON MATING

When a female chimpanzee is in heat, her genitals become red and swollen—a sure sign to would-be suitors that the timing is ripe. But female chimps ovulate only about a week, though they are in heat for about six weeks. Males must make the most of their brief genetic window of opportunity. After the baby is born, it may be three or four *years* before she is sexually receptive again.

Human sexuality, like that of our animal ancestors, is one of the few instances where our biology completely bypasses our huge, evolved, grown-up, relatively slow cortex. The sex drive is perhaps even more powerful than other survival instincts, such as those to eat, sleep, and watch *ER* on Thursday nights. (In experiments, rats given the choice of food or mating would sometimes starve to death while continuing to have sex.) Hormones give our bodies the chance to say *yes! yes! yes!* when our common sense says *let's wait*, or *maybe not*, or even *no!*

Admittedly, the classic contract between males and females (unspoken, but as old as time)—"In exchange for sex, I'll feed you and the kids [procreation and survival with a capital P and S!]"—has changed. Women can get their own jobs, go on welfare, hit the supermarket. So the deal has gotten lopsided in terms of what they "need" from guys. Even the fundamental elixir of life—sperm—can be acquired at the local fertility clinic or the local singles bar.

The availability of sperm has long been a male issue. Reproductively, women have always held most of the biological cards, but now more than ever. Even the Bible says it's a wise child who knows his own father. More recently, in a study done twenty years ago, 50 percent of all pregnant fathers questioned who the dad was. Today there's even a billboard on buses that says, "Question Dad? Try DNA Testing." Nowadays, biologically a mom is still crucial, but the whole biological relevance of a man is in jeopardy.

The available employment opportunities, sperm banks, and contraceptives don't mean that it's cool for women to abuse the sexual prerogative any more than it was okay for men to do so. Payback is tacky and time-consuming. Treating a man as a sperm vial in Guccis is sexist and nasty (especially after having accused him of thinking only with his *little* head for all these years). It's outmoded for women to use sexuality as a trap or a weapon. Withholding sex as a way of getting your own way or labeling a wink at work "sexual harassment" are an abuse of power that will eventually cause the oppressed to rise up and overthrow the status quo—been there, done that, got the T-shirt and the scars. Getting even is no longer acceptable or smart; it means short-term pleasure but long-term pain. Never before have human males and females had such a terrific opportunity to figure out a world, domestic, sexual, and emotional order that allows for mutual respect.

In the grown-up world, throwing a temper tantrum like a

little girl is no more acceptable than acting like a teenager with a hard-on seeing life through a spermy green haze. It's crucial in the land of Maturo to know what you want, think about the long term, and respect each other in the morning . . . and, for heaven's sake, use condoms in the meantime.

ON ROARING

A female vervet monkey—like her male counterpart—shrieks the moment she spots a predator. Her ear-piercing cry warns others of the danger. It's a gut reaction—pure fear. Instantly, and without question, she gets the point across. Monkeys on "lookout" are the troop's early-warning system and play a large role in the survival of the whole group.

Human females often see themselves as guardians of the pack and need to warn of threat by "shrieking," too. In other words, they react *emotionally* to what they perceive as imminent "danger." The problem is, these days "danger" is likely to be the threat of loneliness, divorce, alienation, boredom, and abandonment—not a python slithering through the jungle. Remember, guys tend to view *emotional outbursts* as a flashing red light. Warning! Watch your back! So difficulties arise when the "shrieking" is one-on-one with a man who views emotion as the enemy. A woman's emotional outburst is likely to evoke the ancient, instantaneous gut-level response of days really long ago, igniting the fight-or-flight response. She yells, "How could you?!" and he thinks, "Danger, Will Robinson! I'm outta here."

Whoops—now she's really furious, scared, and alarmed, so the shrieking heightens in decibels, intensity, and duration. He not only *runs*, he hides and remembers to avoid this situation at all costs. It's too dangerous and makes him *really* anxious. So much for a meeting of the minds! Is it any wonder that men and women have problems with conflict resolution? Their styles are diametrically opposed.

When it comes to communication, women consider themselves experts. But *effective* communication means making sure the signal is received. Communication *isn't* about talking long or even loud until someone listens; it's about figuring out how best to be *heard* and *understood.* That means getting specific, not emotional, talking less and listening more, thinking first and speaking second, and knowing exactly what you want.

The reason communication is so scary for human beings is that, by definition, it implies *change.* If everything is okay as is, you don't need to say anything. When a woman says to a man, "We need to talk," he knows she is unhappy with the status quo and wants *him* to change, that's he's done something or *is* something wrong! Change in a relationship is both inevitable and very scary. The joke is, women marry men expecting to change them, and men marry women expecting them to stay exactly the same. Jiminy cricket! Talk about opposites attracting, then aggravating the heck out of each other! Both parties see any unanticipated change of behavior or request for a change as a cause for anxiety: If you've changed, have your feelings for me changed, too? Am I still important to you? If you've changed, do I have to change? What if I can't? What if I don't want to?

Roaring says, "I'm hurt," arguments say, "I'm frustrated and I'm angry," but real communication says, "I love you and this doesn't work for me and I want to figure out a way to change it so it will work for both of us." Women need to turn down the volume, reduce the number of words, stop blaming, start listening, and identify specifically and behaviorally what they really want changed. Not "I want more respect or time," but "Let's set up a Thursday-night date where I'll pick something to do this week and you pick something next week."

ON PLUMAGE

Dominant females in a herd of mountain zebras are the *oldest* females in their herd. They obtain their high status, along with the best spot at the watering hole and the sweetest young grass on the plains, by surviving longer than other females. Age, in the animal kingdom, is often synonymous with wisdom, reverence, and respect.

When it comes to human females, particularly *American* human females, the animal world is turned topsy-turvy. *Youth* is a status symbol among women, *females* decorate themselves for males, and a woman's socially acceptable appearance is all about *denying* nature. Human female plumage—what women use to attract men—is about as far from the animal kingdom as it gets. Which is perhaps why there is such conflict, and conflicting emotions, between men and women on the subject of the way women look.

A female friend of mine from South America proudly displays a great amount of body hair. Since she lives in a racially mixed society in which being "pure bred" is synonymous with being "white bread," and since Caucasians anthropomorphically have more body hair than blacks, being hairy implies "whiter," which is considered classy. For her, status is being as hairy as possible, including hair-covered legs, upper lip, and armpits. The point here is that cultures and eras, as well as sexes, vary greatly and arbitrarily when it comes to standards of beauty.

The current American ideal of feminine beauty—large breasts, tiny body, baby-blond hair, waxed legs, plucked eyebrows, flat tummies, perky buns, an unwrinkled face, unsagging skin, and a designer wardrobe updated each season (think Barbie doll)—is, in short, an impossible standard for most women to achieve and a completely impossible standard for any woman to maintain for any length of time. Women are convinced that men will find them attractive if they are under twenty, have a "C" cup or larger, and are starving, even though men maintain it just ain't so. I don't think the conflict is over skinny versus zaftig; I think it's young versus old.

Normal aging wrinkles skin, puts on pounds, and loosens muscle tone. Gravity is not our friend. Trying to look perpetually young and unblemished is hard work, not to mention entirely futile. No wonder women are so angry (not to mention *hungry*)!

The question is: Is this really what men want, or what women *think* men want? Men have always defined the ideal of what's beautiful, so viewing today's absurd contradictory messages to women about how to look could be seen as an ongoing, historically based means for men to control women. It's just like in the jungle when the Alpha male would determine his choice for his consort, as would an emperor or a rock star. That's not new or surprising. But presumably a male animal has made his choice, consciously or unconsciously, on the basis of continuing the species—good child-bearing material and markings, wide hips, strong bones, healthy teeth, and pelt. Okay, so today big breasts are still valued. But getting milk out of silicone bottles? (Yeah, I'm just making a point here. I know implants don't usually affect the ability to lactate . . . but you get the picture, yes?)

Today, with everything a woman has to do to be "beautiful"

and fight time, gravity, and comfort to attract a male, she has less time and energy to compete head-to-head (or pedicured toe-to-toe) with men in the workplace. Women aren't allowed to age (check out Hugh Downs versus Barbara Walters) or get fat, saggy, or grumpy. Hmmmm . . . all he has to do is shower, clip his fingernails, and wear a white shirt, gray suit, and power tie.

I'm not trying to change society here (okay, well, maybe I am), but rather to suggest that succumbing blindly to a male-conceived version of female beauty—particularly the notion that the only attractive woman is a *young* woman—is guaranteeing a lifetime of self-doubt. Why go there? Instead, women need to take a page from the book of being male and decide who we are and who we want to be, with some other self-definition besides a perfect physiology and the kind of men we attract.

Women aren't gorgeous Venus's-flytraps, artificially luring men to their deaths. We are more than our packaging, and if we can redirect (at least in terms of pregnancy) our biological imperative of being fertile and pregnant to a *choice*, we can resist the temptation to *look* like we're always prepared to be young, fertile, mindless, and untouched by experience.

ON GOING FOR THE KILL

A lioness crouches in the grassy camouflage of the African plains waiting for the perfect moment to strike. As soon as she sees a weak, isolated, or distracted animal, she lunges and, along with other females in her pride, takes down a zebra or a gazelle or a wildebeest. Females hunt for survival—to feed their cubs, themselves, and the male lions in the pride, who usually wait till all the dirty work is done before strolling over for a bite to eat.

Human females "hunt," i.e., bring home the bacon instead of the wildebeest, for similar reasons—to feed their young and themselves and contribute to the well-being of the whole pride. Women have also learned men's dirty little secret: Making money is *fun*. Not every day, all the time, but it feels good to have someone value what you do.

Most women still have a love/hate relationship with money. They want to make the big bucks so they have security. Money is a way to buy independence and feel competitive (if I'm not so young or so beautiful, at least I can be rich), but making lots of money often results in a woman feeling unfeminine—especially if she makes significantly more than her man. Women hide money, they don't talk about it with other women, they use money to make themselves more attractive to men by spending it on clothes, cosmetic surgery, spa weekends.

Or women don't spend money at all, squirreling it away for that rainy day when their man ups and leaves and they are left to fend for themselves and their children. For women, money is much more than inert green stuff used to trade one commodity for another. For women, money is security, power, safety, freedom, dominance, and independence all rolled into one big (yikes!) bank account. It's being able to take care of yourself and not need anybody—a way of being mother, father, husband, and lover to yourself by supplying food, allowance, gifts, a home, security, and fun.

Being self-reliant as a woman is a whole new, scary, lovely place. Virginia Woolf said women need a room of their own—today's woman can own the house and rent out rooms, but is the price tag so threatening to the traditional role of a man that she is always alone?

Men and women view money completely differently, which is why so many couples fight over a symbolic piece of green

stuff. Men see money as life's report card, women see money as
security—either because her man has it and will take care of her
or leave it to her, or because *she* has it, which creates both security and insecurity, as we have discussed. Women also see money
as a means to attract men with money. Yet women with money
don't trust men *without* money. It's a double standard that
demeans men, women, *and* money. Women still have a ways to
go to reach parity with men in money matters, which isn't surprising since they've had direct access for such a short period of
time, but in the meantime, females have to let go of the notion
of money as "allowance" or a symbol of power and status—traditional *male* trappings. To do that, women have to work, make
their own money, feel the power and limitations, and reduce the
almighty dollar down to a two-and-a-half-by-six-inch piece of
rag paper.

Okay, so what are some of the differences between men and
women beyond private parts? What about *public* parts? I've just
spent a whole book showing how the wiring differs behaviorally.
Scientists have finally affirmed what we have suspected, noticed,
and commented on for a very long time: Beyond the obvious, some
male/female behavioral differences can be explained phylogenically
and physiologically rather than psychologically or sociologically. The
astute among you will undoubtedly ask which came first, the behavior or the brain, but for the time being, we currently understand
that, as compared to females, men are considered to be:

✦ LESS INTUITIVE. The old corpus callosum that connects the right and left hemispheres is less well-
developed in men, which allows women to juggle kids,
cooking, cleaning, and carpooling more easily.

✦ MORE FOCUSED. Fewer fibers in the corpus callosum means there's less "cross talk." Men tend to focus on one, and only one, thing at a time, so a guy can seemingly not hear a crying baby, ringing phone, or foot-tapping spouse while engrossed in the sports page. (And you thought he was just being insensitive . . .)

✦ MORE GRUMPY. The male brain, initially larger than a female's, increases the probability that he'll be a grumpy old man. Yeah, size counts—but so do efficiency and testosterone, which slow down as men age.

✦ LESS EMOTIONAL. There are eight times more neurons associated with sadness in a female brain than there are in a male brain. This undoubtedly explains the higher incidence of depression in women than men, although I still think the best definition of depression is anger turned inward, and women are allowed few ways to acknowledge, let alone express, anger. Let me tell you a story. Last night I went to a movie with a couple of friends. My *female* friend sobbed throughout the movie. At the final credits, I turned to my *male* friend and asked, "Did you cry?" He proudly said, "Not for a minute." We went out into the lobby and he said, "This movie really makes me mad. The director tried to pull my chain, and when I felt like crying, I really resisted it . . ." I'm thinking, wow, he censored his feelings, but to censor them he had to *recognize* them first. So much for brain size and shape.

◆ MORE AGGRESSIVE. The male brain idles in the limbic
system, which is an older, more action-oriented, less
verbal part of the brain. Which is why guys often have
more of a "take-charge" personality than women do.

◆ LESS VERBAL. The male focus is more left-brained
than right-brained, which means guys aren't as verbally
tuned in as women are.

◆ BETTER AT VISION. Both in the dark and three-
dimensionally, men tend to see better than women;
they can find enemies and cars in the dark, park better,
and throw a spear straight and true.

◆ WORSE AT HEARING. It's not just his intense ability
to focus that makes him *not* hear the baby crying.
In general, men don't hear as well as women do.

So a blue brain is slightly different from a pink brain, sorta,
or at least it seems to give some basis to being less judgmental and
biased about male/female behavior. But what do we really know,
given all of this impressive new data? In spite of it all, for perhaps
the first time in human history, there's not a clear definition of
what it means to be male and what it means to be female once you
get past genitalia. Once you get past penis and vagina, what defines
us as men and women? Not hair on your head, not hair on your
body, not clothing, not bank account, not ability to take care of
children or not take care of children, not willingness to go to work
or not go to work, not wearing pink shirts or a diamond stud in
your ear. Which is the point of this book. It's not about being

"male" or "female" and following a role, it's about being *human*. It's about figuring out who you are, what you want, and what your options are. And understanding it not only about yourself, but about your partner as well.

If we can understand who we are, what we feel, what we want—and communicate it in a way that another person can understand—we actually have the potential of being truly human with one another. We're *not* animals—we don't have a rutting season, our lives are not mean, short, brutish, and nasty, we've evolved language, we make quantum leaps, we have a will, we can make choices—so whatever animals do isn't going to work for humans anymore. Ultimately, biology is *not* destiny, we're *not* from separate planets. But men and women are unique, we are diverse. In the millennium, *diversity* is the human destiny.

The difference between male and female within a species is presumably much less than any difference between males of different species. The newest information from the genetic front says that there are fewer than fifty—yeah, *fifty*—genes that separate humans from chimps. If we're talking about such a small percentage of material resulting in such humongous differences, maybe it's time to understand the differences and celebrate the similarities.

Recently I was walking down the street and saw a couple quietly talking together with their three-year-old backed up against both Mommy's and Daddy's legs. The child was calmly checking out the world, and in that moment I was reminded of a truth that's bigger than biology or brain size or evolution: The ability of human beings to comfort, aid, and love one another in a complex and sometimes hostile world is a miracle to be devoutly fostered. If we can understand, accept, and negotiate, we can find a bit of serenity and safety in our lives. If we can be civilized with one another, the jungle becomes a great deal less dangerous.

QUANTUM

MEN

Think of one advantage to being a woman.

Think of one advantage to being a man.

Ask yourself if you treat or would treat a son differently than a daughter.

Ask yourself what kind of woman you would be if you came back as the opposite sex.

Be specific with what you think is your strongest attribute and your greatest liability.

WOMEN

Ask yourself, if you were a man, what would you do differently?

Be specific in terms of what kind of work you would do if you were going to support yourself for the rest of your life.

What do you think is the coolest thing about being a man?

What is your favorite thing about being a woman?

What single word describes your style?

Write a listing of what you would do differently if you won the lottery.

LEAPS

ACKNOWLEDGMENTS

THIS BOOK FOCUSES on a lot of Alpha males and how they act in the wild. As a female trying to sort it all out, I, like most females, found myself dependent on the cooperative activities of a group of females who possess all the Alpha characteristics with some estrogen thrown in.

Mary Hogan: Talk about your hunting and gathering skills, from surfing the Net to catching my elusive concepts, I couldn't and wouldn't have done it without you. You held my hand, polished my ideas, researched *and* challenged my notions. Can we do it again on the next one?

Joni Evans: Every group needs that strong, knowledgeable female who's seen Alphas come and go and possesses the wisdom and kindness to counsel the novice. In my case, she tames my wilder impulses without stifling my spirit of adventure, and, as always, is the one who sees my prose and ideas without makeup, so I don't have to publicly embarrass myself.

Barbara Marks: Communication in the tribe is an important part of survival. When it comes to the dog-eat-dog world of commerce, trusting the person who warns, celebrates, and gives the all-clear sign while encouraging you to venture forth into the wider world is crucial. That's Barbara. She has also served as a continuing source of enthusiasm, energy, plane reservations, calm thoughts, and publicity.

Meg Drislane: Animals can work on instinct; humans often need to be reminded of what has come before and the rules that must be followed to maintain the integrity of the species. In the jungle of syntax, logic, and consistency (or its nemesis), someone has to rein in the impulses of the overexuberant. Her clarity, kindness, consistency, and speed accomplished this without hurting my feelings.

Bob Mecoy: Okay, so we've finally gotten to the Alpha male part. The guy who can rule wisely and well without stifling the energy of the tribe (or in this case, the scribe) is truly evolved. Talk about lucking out: an editor who is smart, fast, articulate, and *male*. I knew I was on the right track when I could make you blush. Thanks for your strength, your courtesy, expertise, and tact. Saying that I called your and every other guy's bluff on not only the big stuff but the little stuff warmed the cockles of my heart.

Peter Fornatale: Okay—so as an Alpha-in-training, you're a lovely combination of efficiency, charm, and information. Don't let the testosterone get you down.

Chip, Steve, and Andy: To the ultimate Alphas, your presence and support continue to be a source of strength and glee.

All you guys, Alphas to Zetas, who've called the program and shared your deepest, darkest, silliest, most profound, coolest, and nastiest thoughts with me. In helping y'all I've come to better understand myself, men, women, passion, pride, prejudice, and primping. This book is about what I've learned.

DR. JOY BROWNE has been an archaeologist, a med school student, and an engineer in the space program and has had her own private psychology practice. A licensed clinical psychologist, she received the 1998 American Psychological Association's President's Award for contributions to the field. Voted Best Female Talk Show Host for the last two years by the National Association of Talk Show Hosts, Dr. Joy's radio program is heard on more than 300 stations in the United States and Canada and her television show can be seen throughout the country. She is the author of six books, including *The Nine Fantasies That Will Ruin Your Life* and the best-selling *Dating for Dummies*.